# RELIGION IN LIFE CURRICULUM

### Edited by Edward A. Fitzpatrick, Ph.D.

I0150665

# FIFTH GRADE TEACHERS PLAN BOOK
# AND MANUAL

BOOK OF THE HOLY CHILD (Grade One)

LIFE OF MY SAVIOR (Grade Two)

LIFE OF THE SOUL (Grade Three)

BEFORE CHRIST CAME (Grade Four)

THE VINE AND THE BRANCHES (Grade Five)

THE MISSAL (Grade Six)

HIGHWAY TO GOD (Grades Seven and Eight)

---

Accompanying this Series is the RELIGION IN LIFE CURRICULUM for grades one to six and PRACTICAL PROBLEMS IN RELIGION for grades seven and eight.

*Religion in Life Curriculum*

# Fifth Grade Teachers Plan Book and Manual

**A School Sister of Notre Dame**

*Member of the Faculty of the Diocesan Teachers*
*College, St. Paul, Minnesota*

Designed for use with the
HIGHWAY TO HEAVEN SERIES
of Catechism Textbooks

ST. AUGUSTINE ACADEMY PRESS
HOMER GLEN, ILLINOIS

Nihil obstat:

GEORGE J. ZISKOVSKY,
Censor deputatus

Imprimatur:

✠ JOHN G. MURRAY,
Archbishop of St. Paul

March 15, 1934

This book was originally published in 1935 by The Bruce Publishing Company.
This edition reprinted in 2018 by St. Augustine Academy Press.
ISBN: 978-1-64051-036-4

# INTRODUCTION

In this grade the center of interest is the Church. From the very first grade, where the redemptive plan was presented to the child in its simplest form, the Church has been a matter of continuing and growing interest until in this grade it becomes the center of interest. In the subsequent grades it continues to be very important, and in the eighth grade a comprehensive, doctrinal view of the Church is presented, rounding out the whole study.

It has been pointed out frequently that in this series Christ is the foundation. It was the Messianic idea that guided our study of the history of God's chosen people, and it is Christ in the Church — His Mystical Body — that gives meaning to the study of the history of the Christian era. To separate in any way Christ and His Church is not to be faithful to the true spirit of Catholicism. These two grades, too, form a larger unity in their treatment of the idea of sacrifice under the old and the new dispensation, with the anticipation of the new in the sacrifice of Melchisedec.

The title of the textbook is significant, *The Vine and the Branches*. It is, of course, based on Christ's words:

"I am the true vine: and My Father is the husbandman. Every branch in Me that beareth not fruit He will take away: and every one that beareth fruit He will purge it, that it may bring forth more fruit.

"Now you are clean by reason of the word, which I have spoken to you.

"Abide in Me, and I in you. As the branch cannot bear fruit of itself, unless it abide in the vine, so neither can you, unless you abide in Me.

"I am the vine; you the branches; he that abides in Me, and

v

I in him, the same beareth much fruit: for without Me you can do nothing.

"If anyone abide not in Me, he shall be cast forth as a branch, and shall wither, and they gather him up, and cast him into the fire, and he burneth.

"If you abide in Me, and My words abide in you, you shall ask whatever you will, and it shall be done unto you" (John xv. 1-6).

These should be the central thought of the study of the life of the Church in this grade. Each lesson should go back to the central idea of the Church, the means of salvation. The emphasis to be given in this grade is indicated in the editor's introduction to the textbook.

There is a wealth of pedagogical suggestions in this manual, and the teachers are especially urged to read carefully the introductory comments to the user of the book and to the "reverend instructor." These suggestions need not be repeated here.

The teacher will not assume that the child is approaching the thought of the Church for the first time. She will recall that the Church is the central factor in the Christian Scheme of Redemption, and that Christ lives in the Church. Unit IV of *The Life of the Soul* (pp. 81–87) deals solely with the "Church of Christ." In Book IV, *Before Christ Came,* and in the manual as well, the lesson of respect for priests is taught as well as the necessity to contribute to their support and to the support of the Church. Many questions are given to test the child's knowledge and attitude toward the Church. Nor should the teacher fail to look forward to the detailed discussions in the book for the seventh and eighth grades, *The Highway to God* (pp. 225–240, pp. 358–382, and pp. 383–390). More significant than this is the finely spiritual conception of the Church as well as the indication of the practical duty of Catholics toward it which pervades the whole series. This the teacher must communicate.

The spirit of the teacher will count much in this presentation of the life of Christ in the Church. She can do no better than keep as her guiding thoughts those in the paragraph which concludes *The Life of the Church:*

"Normally, nobody comes to the Father save by the Son, Jesus Christ; in point of fact, nobody finds Christ except in the Church. In the third century St. Cyprian had already pointed out, in a striking condensation, that, since the coming of the Lord, 'nobody can any longer have God for his Father who has not the Church for his mother.' More than a thousand years later, when enmeshed in a tangle of cunning questions, St. Joan of Arc, one of the noblest creatures who ever did honour to the human race, and one of the most simply, the most genuinely Christian, replied to her judges: 'It seems to me that our Lord and the Church are all one; you ought not to make a difficulty of that.' "[1]

EDWARD A. FITZPATRICK

The Catechetical Institute,
Marquette University.

---

[1]Pierre Rousselot, S.J., L. de Grandmaison, S.J., V. Huby, S.J., Alexandre Brou, M. C. D'Arcy, S.J., *The Life of the Church* (New York: Lincoln Mac-Veagh, Sheed and Ward, 1932).

## EDITOR'S NOTE TO THE REPRINTED EDITION:

In reassembling this *Religion in Life Curriculum*, we thought it best to include excerpts from the curriculum overview volume, titled *Curriculum in Religion*, which was published in 1931 as the basis for development of the fleshed-out Teachers Plan Book and Manual before you. In that original volume, the entire curriculum for first through eighth grades were laid out in basic outline form, with attention given to the main focus, goals and resources for each grade. You may find that some of the resources listed in these excerpts did not find their way into the current manual. However, we felt it would be helpful to the teacher (or parent) to see a summary of the intended vision for the current year.

In the appendix found at the rear of this volume, we have also provided a comprehensive listing of all the recommended resources found in this manual, to which we have added notations showing the most frequently used and/or most helpful resources, as well as those which can be found online.

Lastly, please note that most of the recommended student readings (that is, those which would have been found in the various school readers listed throughout the student text) have been assembled and printed under one cover in the new *Magnificat Readers* which accompany this series. In addition, we have done our best to find and scan the pages of *The Catholic School Journal* and *The Journal of Religious Instruction* recommended herein; find these on our website at www.staapress.com/hth-teacher-resources.

*Lisa Bergman*

*St. Augustine Academy Press*
*March 2018*

# CONTENTS

*The following section is an excerpt from the book "A Curriculum in Religion," included for the convenience of teachers as a way of familiarizing themselves with the basic goals laid out for the Religion in Life Curriculum for the Fifth Grade.*

# RELIGION IN GRADE V

## Main Interest: Church History

THE center of interest in the fifth grade is the history of the Church told in a series of biographies of popular saints, and other Catholic leaders. It is especially important here that nothing shall be taught which needs to be unlearned. The teacher might read with profit for a general point of view Belloc's *The Catholic Church and History.*

### Point of View

It is possible at this level to give a child a historical sense of the greatness of the Church's followers. It is this sense of the greatness, the stability, and the security of the Church that the students will get through the biographies. The teacher must feel this, else it cannot be communicated very well. A paragraph in Father Guilday's *An Introduction to Church History* is copied here for the teacher's guidance:

"Out of it all — out of the tremendous past of the Church, out of the certainties and uncertainties that crowd its pages, one fact looms high in historical value: if ever there was a power or an institution on earth which should long since have perished from the memory of man, that power and that institution is the Catholic Church. What has not been done to destroy it? A hundred times in the past twenty centuries has the Church of God stood on the verge of utter collapse. So has it seemed to human eyes. But the standard set up in the midst of the nations remains forever erect, strengthening its adherents with the unfaltering assurance that their Faith is founded upon a rock, solid and impregnable. In its infancy in the Jewish synagogues of a dying Israel, amid the unspeakable perils of the Roman persecutions, in the depths of the catacombs, under the dead weight of the barbarian blight, in the subtle toils of feudal encroachments, in the presence of the mighty tyranny of a new Cæsarism, in the dark night of the cleavage during the sixteenth century, amid the enmities of Protestant nations and the uncertain friendships of Catholic nations, down to these days of our own, the struggle for liberty of action and independence for spiritual conquest has never ceased. But through it all and in it all and in spite of all that has been attempted to thwart the onward march of her progress, the Church has been victorious. This, then, is the foremost lesson of her history: the unconquerable stability of the Catholic Faith."

There is a quotation in Father Guilday's book from Père Delehaye's *Legends of the Saints* that might very well guide the teacher in the selection of her material for the biographies. It is:

"Historical criticism, when applied to the lives of the saints, has had certain results which are in no way surprising to those who are accustomed to handle documents and to interpret inscriptions, but which have had a somewhat disturbing effect on the mind of the general public. . . . If you suggest that the biographer of a saint has been unequal to his task, or that he has not professed to write as a historian, you are accused of attacking the saint himself, who, it appears, is too powerful to allow himself to be compromised by an indiscreet panegyrist. If, again, you venture to express doubt concerning certain marvelous incidents repeated by the author on insufficient evidence, although well calculated to enhance the glory of the saint, you are at once suspected of lack of faith. You are told you are introducing the spirit of rationalism into history, as though in questions of fact it were not above all things essential to weigh the evidence. How often has not an accusation of destructive criticism been flung, and men treated as iconoclasts, whose sole object has been to appraise at their true value the documents which justify our attitude of veneration, and who are only too happy when able to declare that one of God's friends has been fortunate enough to find a historian worthy of his task."

## Outline of Main Topics

The content of the fifth grade will center around the history of the Church. Starting out with the life of Christ as the foundation of the life of the Church, and supplementing it with the lives and statements of Paul and Peter, the pupil will then study the great personalities in the development of the Church in biographical form. Each personality is selected especially for the points listed in the detailed syllabus which supplements this course of study. Here as in the fourth grade the teacher will provide if the text does not, the historical situation in which the character acted, and in this way emphasize historical backgrounds and secure historical continuity.

A. *Founding of Church*
   1. Christ, the Foundation
   2. St. Peter, the Rock
B. *Early Development*
   1. St. Paul
   2. Timothy
   3. St. Stephen and Other Early Martyrs
   4. St. Augustine and the Church Fathers
   5. Council of Nicea
   6. Conversion of Constantine
C. *Development of Monasticism*
   1. St. Anthony
   2. St. Benedict
D. *The Crusades*
   1. Mohammed and Mohammedans
   2. Pope Urban and the Crusades
   3. Lay Leaders
E. *Development of Papacy*
   1. Gregory
   2. Innocent
F. *Great Saints of Middle Ages*
   1. St. Thomas Aquinas
   2. St. Dominic
   3. St. Francis of Assisi
   4. St. Bernard
G. *The Revolution*
   1. St. Ignatius Loyola
   2. The Council of Trent
H. *Founding of Schools*
   1. The Popes and the Universities
   2. Blessed de la Salle
   3. The Church and Art

## Quotations

The quotations in this grade center on the nature and characteristics of the Church. Here as in preceding grades the quotations will not be taught as unrelated quotations assigned for memorizing, but significant statements conveniently summarizing some fact or the significant basis of doctrines. In this grade particularly, the teacher should be satisfied if the child gets the fundamental idea. Theological discussion is not desirable or necessary. Subsequent study in this curriculum provides for recalling to mind these passages within the elementary-school period. The significant quotations are:

"For if the blood of goats and of oxen, and the ashes of an heifer being sprinkled, sanctify such as are defiled, to the cleansing of the flesh:

"How much more shall the blood of Christ, Who by the Holy Ghost offered Himself unspotted unto God, cleanse our conscience from dead works, to serve the living God?" (Heb. ix. 12–14.)

"Amen, amen, I say unto you: He that believeth in Me, hath everlasting life.

I am the bread of life.

Your fathers did eat manna in the desert, and are dead.

This is the bread which cometh down from heaven that if any man eat of it, he may not die.

I am the living bread which came down from heaven.

If any man eat of this bread, he shall live for ever; and the bread that I will give, is My flesh, for the life of the world.

The Jews, therefore, strove among themselves, saying: How can this man give us His flesh to eat?

Then Jesus said to them: Amen, amen, I say unto you: Except you eat the flesh of the Son of man, and drink His blood, you shall not have life in you.

He that eateth My flesh, and drinketh My blood, hath everlasting life: and I will raise him up in the last day.

For My flesh is meat indeed: and My blood is drink indeed.

He that eateth My flesh, and drinketh My blood, abideth in Me, and I in him.

As the living Father hath sent Me, and I live by the Father; so he that eateth Me, the same also shall live by Me.

This is the bread that came down from heaven. Not as your fathers did eat manna, and are dead. He that eateth this bread, shall live for ever.

These things He said, teaching in the synagogue, in Capharnaum" (John vi. 47–60).

"And Jesus coming, spoke to them, saying: All power is given to Me in heaven and in earth.

Going therefore, teach ye all nations; baptizing them in the name of the Father, and of the Son, and of the Holy Ghost.

Teaching them to observe all things whatsoever I have commanded you: and behold I am with you all days, even to the consummation of the world" (Matt. xxviii. 18–20).

"But you shall receive the power of the Holy Ghost coming upon you, and you shall be witnesses unto Me in Jerusalem, and in all Judea, and Samaria, and even to the uttermost part of the earth" (Acts i. 8).

"And they were all filled with the Holy Ghost, and they began to speak with divers tongues, according as the Holy Ghost gave them to speak" (Acts ii. 4).

"And all the temptation being ended, the devil departed from Him for a time" (Luke iv. 13).

"You have not chosen Me: but I have chosen you; and have appointed you, that you should go, and should bring forth fruit; and your fruit should remain: that whatsoever you shall ask of the Father in My name, He may give it you" (John xv. 16).

"And when you fast, be not as the hypocrites, sad. For they disfigure their faces, that they may appear unto men to fast. Amen I say to you, they have received their reward" (Matt. vi. 16).

"I am the vine; you the branches: he that abideth in Me, and I in him, the same beareth much fruit: for without Me you can do nothing" (John xv. 5).

"He said, therefore, to them again: Peace be to you. As the Father hath sent Me, I also send you.

When He had said this, He breathed on them; and He said to them: Receive ye the Holy Ghost.

Whose sins you shall forgive, they are forgiven them; and whose *sins* you shall retain, they are retained" (John xx. 21–23).

"When, therefore, they had dined, Jesus saith to Simon Peter: Simon, son of John, lovest thou Me more than these?

He saith to Him: Yea, Lord, Thou knowest that I love Thee. He saith to him: Feed My lambs.

He saith to him again: Simon, *son* of John, lovest thou Me? He saith to Him: Yea, Lord, Thou knowest that I love Thee. He saith to him: Feed My lambs.

He said to him the third time: Simon, son of John, lovest thou Me? Peter was grieved, because He had said to him the third time: Lovest thou Me? And he said to Him: Lord, Thou knowest all things: Thou knowest that I love Thee. He said to him: Feed My sheep" (John xxi. 15–17).

"Jesus saith to them: But Whom do you say that I am?

Simon Peter answered and said: Thou art Christ, the Son of the living God.

And Jesus answering, said to him: Blessed art thou, Simon Bar-Jona: because flesh and blood hath not revealed it to thee, but My Father Who is in heaven.

And I say to thee: That thou art Peter; and upon this rock I will build My Church, and the gates of hell shall not prevail against it.

And I will give to thee the keys of the kingdom of heaven. And whatsoever thou shalt bind upon earth, it shall be bound also in heaven: And whatsoever thou shalt loose on earth, it shall be loosed also in heaven" (Matt. xvi. 15–19).

## Activities

The stories of the Old Testament offer excellent opportunities for spontaneous dramatization in the classroom, and for a more formal literary dramatization. Suggestions are contained in *Practical Aids for Catholic Teachers* by Sister Aurelia and Father Kirsch (pp. 234–238). Suggestive dramatizations are offered (pp. 242–245) of:

Adoration of the Shepherd
Adoration of the Magi
Jesus Blessing Little Children
St. Francis and the Wolf

St. Francis Preaching to the Birds
Blessed Herman Joseph and the Infant Jesus
Pantomime — Blessed Herman Joseph*

The student will prepare a booklet on his patron saint in this grade. He will also prepare one on some major saint, presenting orally to the class, toward the end of the semester or year, a summary of what he learned. Sand-table projects, posters, calendars, booklets, plays, stories, collection of poems, pictures, even movies, furnish fresh methods of approach, or methods of reënforcing more conventional methods of learning.

## Pictures

The texts in this grade both basal and supplementary will have good pictures. Special attention is called to the pictures by Gibhard Fügel in a German school bible, *Bergmann's Katholische Schulbibel*, (Muller). The following pictures with others, besides being valuable in themselves, will serve as an additional interest for the topics of the grade:

*St. John and the Virgin Mary* — Plockhorst
*St. John Evangelist* — Correggio
*Sistine Madonna* — Raphael
*Madonna of the Chair* — Raphael
*Mater Dolorosa* — Guido Reni
*Madonna in Adoration* — Correggio
*Immaculate Conception* — Murillo
*Coronation of the Virgin* — Fra Angelico
*Christ Washing Peter's Feet* — Ford Brown
*Denial of St. Peter* — Harrack

---

*The steps in analyzing a story either in preparation for a dramatization or for writing a biography are illustrated in the article by Miss Margaret Canty, entitled "Joseph the Dreamer," published in the March, 1931, issue of the CATHOLIC SCHOOL JOURNAL.

*The Ascension* — Hoffmann
*St. John and St. Peter* — Durer
*St. Peter Walking on the Sea* — Giotto
*St. Peter in Prison* — Raphael
*Deliverance of St. Peter* — Lippi
*Crucifixion of St. Peter* — Lippi
*Martyrdom of St. Stephen* — Fra Angelico
*St. Mark Rescuing a Slave* — Tintoretto
*Christian Martyrs* — Gerome
*Paul Shipwrecked* — Doré
*St. Paul and St. Mark* — Durer
*Apparition of the Cross to Constantine* — Pupils of Raphael
*Victory of Constantine the Great over Maxentius*
*Descent from the Cross* — Rubens
*Crucifixion* — Martini
*Christ Bearing His Cross* — Hoffmann
*Last Communion of St. Jerome* — Damenichino
*Madonna with St. Jerome* — Correggio
*Vision of St. Augustine* — Botticelli
*Sir Galahad* — Watts
*Tapestry Weavers* — Velasques
*Jesus Healing the Ten Lepers* — Edwin Long
*Cathedral of Rheims*
*Tomb of Dante*
*Cathedral of Milan*
*St. Anthony of Padua* — Murrillo
*Poverty* — Giotto
*Group of Monks* — Pinturicchio
*St. Peter's*, Rome
*Francis Xavier*
*The Communicants*
*Pope Pius X*
*The Last Supper* — Da Vinci

## Religious Vocabulary

Special care must be taken to see that the child's
religious vocabulary is increased in connection partic-

ularly with the main topic of the grade, and that the new words are taught as the need develops and in the actual situation. Care should be taken to review words previously learned and to be sure a correct meaning is given to them on the child's own level. The words should grow in connotation as his religious knowledge and experience increases. Words that will generally be taught in this grade are:

| | | |
|---|---|---|
| emperor | Mahometan | conception |
| apostles | infidels | ascension |
| converts | saints | resurrection |
| pagans | universities | baptized |
| Constantine | apostacy | martyrs |
| doctrines | Jesuits | heretics |
| monks | hospitals | cathedral |
| barbarians | Vatican | monastic |
| monasteries | doctors | crusades |
| Mohammedans | crucify | Lepanto |
| chivalry | Holy Ghost | immaculate |
| indulgences | martyrdom | atrocities |
| vows | council | religious orders |
| missionaries | patriarch | Franciscans |
| Dominicans | migration | reign of terror |
| sects | schism | concordat |
| infallibility | | |

Each teacher will be required to make up her specific lists for her specific children. No stress need be placed on the spelling of these words. They may be left on the board for reference.

### Poems

The poems suggested for the fifth grade carrying along the fundamental idea of the curriculum and furnishing reënforcement for the central interest of this grade are:

*Not Myrrh nor Frankincense I Bring* — Rev. Francis J. Butler
*Beauty in Common Things* — Minot J. Savage
*Our Birth* — William Wordsworth
*A Prayer* — Edwin Markham
*Be What Thou Seemest*
*Lucy's Rosary* — J. R. Marre
*Lead, Kindly Light* — Cardinal Newman
*Labor*
*Our Life is but a Little Holding, Lent* — George Meredith
*The Power of God* — Thomas Moore
*When Evening Shades are Falling* — Thomas Moore
*The Bluebird* — Father Tabb
*The Precious Blood of Jesus* — Henry Coyle
*St. Joseph's Month* — H. W.
*Proud Boast* — Sister M. Madeleva
*To a Holy Innocent* — Edward F. Garesché, S.J.
*Old Nuns* — James M. Hayes

Additional poems should be used emphasizing the public life of Christ which is the center of interest in this grade. Children should be encouraged to "learn by heart" as many poems as possible. All should be required to learn some; many of the poems should be left to the student's own taste. The more difficult poems will be read to the class by the teachers; some poems will be read for their general idea without detailed study, and some poems will be studied in detail. Poems dealing with the same subject in earlier grades should be recalled to mind after the first reading of new poems. The poems suggested above, with others, are included in *Religious Poems for Children, Intermediate Grades.* (Bruce.)

## Aspirations, Brief Prayers, Meditations

As opportunity offers, the following aspirations or others will be taught. One might be selected and written on the board each month, calling attention to it as opportunity permits. The students might prepare aspirations of their own. We inserted the tenth one on our list as suggestive of others, too, to furnish a basis for the beginning of the practice of meditation.

1. O sweetest Heart of Jesus, I implore that I may ever love Thee more and more.
2. O Mary conceived without sin, pray for us who have recourse to thee.
3. Inflame our hearts with the fire of the Holy Spirit that we may serve Thee with chaste bodies and please Thee with clean hearts.
4. Blessed be the Holy and Immaculate Conception of the Blessed Virgin Mary.
5. Mother of Love, of Sorrow, and of Mercy, pray for us.
6. Savior of the world, have mercy on us.
7. Jesus, my God, I love Thee above all things.
8. Sweet Jesus, be not to me a Judge but a Savior.
9. Holy Spirit, enlighten me.
10. What doth it profit a man if he gain the whole world but suffer the loss of his own soul.

## Prayers

As the child develops, the form of prayers he will learn will change. The form of morning prayer will undoubtedly change from the simplest form to the use of the liturgical prayers of the Church. This will be generally the development. There will be, of course, an increase in the number of prayers, so that by the end of the elementary school the student will be acquainted with the principal prayers of the Church.

1. Morning prayers
2. Evening prayers
3. Grace before meals
4. Grace after meals
5. Act of Contrition
6. Act of Faith
7. Act of Hope
8. Act of Charity
9. Stations of the Cross
10. The Gloria
11. Prayers of thanksgiving and praise from the Psalms
12. The Confiteor
13. Litany of the Saints
14. Prayer before a Crucifix

### Hymns

Hymns are an important factor in reënforcing the general religious instruction and training, valuable for their own content, and, if properly taught, add an element of joy in religious instruction that is quite important. The child should, at the end of instruction, know the great hymns of the Church. For the fifth grade, there is suggested the following to be sung within the voice range of the children:

1. To Christ the King
2. O Sanctissima
3. Holy Patron Thee Saluting
4. Hail, Aloysius, Hail
5. Hail, Glorious St. Patrick
6. Carmel's Little Flower

7. Out of the Depths (De Profundis)
8. Fuel in the Panting Heart of Rome

## Liturgy

In this grade the liturgical vessels and utensils will be studied: The consecrated paten and chalice, the blessed ciborium, lunette, and monstrance, and the thurible or censer, the sanctus bell, the processional cross. This study of the liturgical vessels and utensils will be supplemented by the name and use of the principal liturgical linen. The child should be shown both the vessels and the linen in their actual place on the altar by the priest or assistant using the opportunity for further instruction.

Useful supplementary material for the study of various aspects of the liturgy will be found in Father Dunney's *The Mass* (Macmillan), and Father M. S. MacMahon's *Liturgical Catechism* (Gill & Son, Dublin), and *St. Andrew's Missal*.

## Religious Information

There are certain facts about religious persons, vestments, ceremonies, and institutions that are a part of the equipment of every cultivated person, as well as essential, or at least supplementary, to religious practice. These need to be taught, and specific provision should be made for the instruction.

One is surprised often to find adults who do not know what INRI means, or *Alpha* and *Omega*, or even IHS, why the Mass is said in Latin, or who some prominent character in the Old or New Testament is. The teacher should use every opportunity to give such information whenever she discovers there is need for it. In this grade will be taught, in addition to what the teacher discovers to be the need of the pupil, the following:

*Geography of Palestine in Christ's Day*

A. Main divisions of Palestine
    1. Judea, Samaria, Galilee, Perea
B. Principal Places
    1. Bethlehem, Nazareth
    2. Jerusalem
    3. Bethsaida, Capharnaum, Cana
    4. Damascus
C. The Dead Sea, the Sea of Galilee, and River Jordan
D. Detailed Study of Jerusalem
    1. Gethsemane
    2. Mount of Olives
    3. The Gates
    4. Via Dolorosa
    5. Calvary
E. Practice in Map Drawing

*Facts About New Testament*

A. Language of the New Testament
B. Jewish Life in Christ's Day
    1. The Principal Sects
        *a*) Pharisees
        *b*) Sadducees
C. Official Life
    1. The Scribes
    2. The Sanhedrin
    3. Synagogue
    4. Tribute money

5. The Publicans
D. Historical Background
1. The Roman Empire

Volume IV of Father Hugh Pope's *The Catholic Student's Aids to the Study of the Bible* (second edition, revised) is an authoritative and valuable source of information in the New Testament generally and the Gospels. Its outline will be generally useful.

A specially useful source of questions and answers for this part of the course on religious information is Father John F. Sullivan's *Externals of the Catholic Church, Her Government, Ceremonies, Festivals, Sacramentals and Devotions* (Kenedy), and Father Conway's *The Question Box*. The new *Catholic Dictionary* is specially useful. For reference the *Catholic Encyclopedia* is indispensable.

This heading is placed in the curriculum so that the teacher will realize the relative importance of this informational background to the main purpose, and will not give it undue emphasis at the expense of weightier matters. Information should be given as information.

## Religious Practice

A definite part of the program in every grade is to build up the practice of religion in every grade and have the development cumulative throughout the grades. Wherever teachers see opportunity to build up Catholic practice they should do so. Teachers must not confound the lessons that may be essential and the actual practice in the life of the child. The pupil should understand the importance of interior disposition.

In the assignment to grade, the purpose is to provide

a specific time to see that the practice is established and understood. In some cases the habit will have been established. The cumulative listing of these practices is to emphasize the fact that they are not taught or established once and you are through with them. The practice must continue to be stimulated until it is "securely rooted in the life of the individual."

There should be emphasized in this grade:

1. Morning Prayer
2. Evening Prayer
3. Regular attendance at Mass on Sundays
4. Attendance at Mass on all holydays of obligation
5. Angelus
6. Bowing at the name of Jesus
7. Tipping hat or bowing as one passes a Catholic church
8. Tipping hat when one meets a Priest or Sister or other religious
9. Monthly Communion or more frequently
10. Keeping spirit of Lent by sacrifice
11. Saying Stations of the Cross
12. Practice of saying brief prayers or ejaculations or aspirations in time of temptation
13. Prayer for our parents

### Practical Life

The translation of the religious knowledge, practice, and attitudes in the day-to-day life of the child must always be an objective in religious education. The elevation of the actual daily life of the individual to a supernatural plane will come about through the character of the individual's motivation. This must be a matter of development; the child must be taken, however, where he is. The lines of development are indicated, but the more specific content is left for the experimentation of the first year. A teacher should always take advantage of any actual situation, and should always strive to meet difficulties which her children, as a group, are confronted with, no matter whether it is included in the course of study or not.

1. Do a good turn every day for the love of God.
   a) Daily examination of conscience at night.
   b) Daily specific review of day's thoughts, words, or deeds.
   c) Weekly complete examination of conscience for confession or as a preparation for spiritual Communion.
   d) Daily expiation for the temporal punishment due to sin.
2. Cultivation of virtuous life.
3. Cultivation of school virtues.
4. Promotion of corporal and spiritual works of mercy.

Special attention is directed to the chapters on "The Christian Rule of Life" and "The Christian Daily Exercise" of the *Catechism of Christian Doctrine* approved by the Cardinal, Archbishops, and Bishops of England and Wales, and directed to be used in all their dioceses.

## Christian Doctrine

In this grade the character of the Church, as the Body of Christ, its marks, and attributes are studied in their historical setting. Typical saints are studied in each century, and the fuller significance of the Communion of Saints, the deposit of grace, and the doctrine of indulgences is indicated. The power of the Church to teach and command is noted, as are the particular precepts of the Church that are noted for special attention.

## Texts and Teaching Material

An adequate basal text on the New Testament on the fifth-grade level is not now available. The syllabus contains the detailed outline of the instruction. It is expected that the experience of the first year will give an adequate basis for a text especially prepared for the course written with a biographical emphasis. The following newer texts may prove useful:

*Bible Stories for Children* — Sister Anna Louise
*Bible History of the Old and New Testament with Compendium of Church History* — Sister Anna Louise
*Compendium of Bible and Church History* — Brother Eugene
*Important Events in Church History* — Brother Eugene
*Illustrated Bible History* — Rev. Ignatius Schuster
*A Child's Garden of Religion Stories* — Rev. P. Henry Matimore
*Wonder Stories of God's People* — Rev. P. Henry Matimore
*A Rhymed Alphabet of Saints* — Father Benson, Reginald Balfane, and S. C. Ritchies, (Benziger)[1]
*Little Lives of the Saints for Children* — Th. Berthold's (Benziger)
Catholic Truth Society *Catholic Biographies*, 8 vols. (Herder)

Valuable suggestions may be secured from stories in school readers. A partial list indicating the range as well as technique of the material is given at the end of this grade.

---

[1] All students should own a copy of this. It might be memorized in whole or in part.

RELIGION IN GRADE V

# FIFTH GRADE TEACHER'S PLAN BOOK AND MANUAL

## To You Who Are Teaching *The Vine and the Branches* Use Your Plan Book Regularly

This plan book is intended for your specific use. It may contain many suggestions with which you are already familiar, it is true. In that case it will give you a great deal of satisfaction. On the other hand, you will most probably find much to help you make your religion classes more interesting and vital. The suggestions given for each lesson are the outgrowth of long personal experience and intimate contact with other teachers of religion. They are not intended to hinder you in exercising your ingenuity but rather to help you to organize your work with the least possible loss of time and to assist you in bringing new and interesting material to the classroom each week.

You are urged also to consult the reference frequently for suggested helpful material.

## The End to be Kept in Mind

The end to be achieved according to the method here proposed is not project work, nor booklets, nor plays, nor other interesting activities. All these are but *means* to an end. The end is to present religious truth so interestingly, so convincingly, so full of spirit and life, that it will take hold of the mind and heart and will, and manifest itself eventually in every phase of the child's life.

## The Textbook

A careful study of *The Vine and the Branches* will bring to light the following outstanding features:

1. It brings before the child in narrative form the beginning and growth of the Church, its trials and its triumphs through the ages down to the present day.

2. Through biographies of saints and great leaders of the Church the child is given a historical sense of the greatness of the Church's followers. The "unconquerable stability of the Catholic Faith" is effectively presented.

3. The doctrine is developed naturally from the story (Christ's own method) and in consequence the religious truths (usually presented in a cold, isolated manner, in question-and-answer form) are better understood and more easily applied to life situations.

4. Religious instruction reaches out into every phase of child-life and correlates naturally with every other activity in and out of school; for "Religion is life."

5. There is a distinct and consistent aim at character training viewed as an outgrowth of the teachings of Christ and His Church rather than as a separate function without doctrinal foundation.

6. The latest and best pedagogical methods, which take into consideration the age, ability, and interests of the child, are used, making the study of religion more pleasant, vital, and effective than is possible by the old methods.

## The Units

The book is divided into units or natural divisions that can be easily grasped by the child. The Introductions to the Units usually take a backward look to view what has already been learned and to indicate the connection between past lessons and those to follow. They are the strong links that bind together the various parts into a well-organized, consistent whole. The teacher should strive to keep this purpose in mind and help the children to focus attention from time to time on the history of the Church as a complete picture.

## The Aim of the Week's Lesson

It is important for the teacher to have clearly in mind, as she presents each lesson, the specific aims of the week's work. For that reason the aim is stated in this manual at the beginning of each lesson. With that in mind, the teacher and pupils will know exactly the purpose of the various activities which might otherwise easily deteriorate into work without definite purpose.

## Preparation

The success of each lesson depends largely upon the teacher's preparation. It is, therefore, of the greatest importance that she look over her work for the week, note any suggestions she may desire to carry out, and proceed to gather and prepare the required material. Not every suggested activity need or should be carried out to the letter. If she knows of better or more interesting ways of developing the lesson, she should, by all means, use them.

The activities of the week, if planned ahead of time, will easily fit themselves into the different periods of the day or to a bit of outside study. Frequently the children may be encouraged to carry out directions and find information on their own initiative.

## Approach to the Lesson

The teacher should plan to approach the day's lesson in religion from various angles so as to make the pupils look forward eagerly to further developments. Instead of beginning every morning with, "Now take your books and we shall continue our religion lesson," she may say nothing whatever about the book for the time being, but read a little poem, let us say, that really strikes the keynote of the thought to be developed that day. The poem is discussed and finally the teacher says,

"Now let us see what our book has to say about the subject."
Stories, hymns, and particularly pictures may be used in the
same way. For example, the story "The Cathedral Builders"
could be approached through pictures of great cathedrals of
the world.

## The Story

Ordinarily it will be found most convenient to begin the
week's work with the story itself. However, the story may
serve also as a development of the lesson (as in Lesson 1)
or as a summary at the end of the week, if the lesson is one
that can be developed without the aid of the book. Frequently
the story will have to be read several times. Sometimes it should
be read just for appreciation after all the facts are well known.
The story need not always be read during the religion period,
however. Another period may well be used at times; for
example, the reading period. Sometimes, too, the lesson may
be read at home.

The stories should be made as real as possible. The teacher
should talk about them, help the children over their difficulties,
explain new words, early customs, etc., and keep in mind always
the unifying thought as suggested by the title of the text and
especially by the title of each unit.

## The Questions on the Story

The questions following the story are intended to ascertain
whether the pupils have grasped the lesson. They may be used
also to stimulate thought, by proposing them ahead of time and
having the pupils read quietly to find the answer. Again, the
teacher may use the questions to convince herself that the story
has been read by the pupils at home or during another period,
and that it has been thoroughly understood. They may be used
orally, assigned as written work, or omitted altogether if there
is no further need for them. The omission should not be
frequent, however.

## Topics for Discussion

Such topics as "Ask Yourself," also the quotations and other selections, offer splendid material for character training. The aim of the teacher must be not so much to get the right answer as to direct the children to think for themselves, to recognize their own needs and shortcomings, and most important of all, to acquire the right viewpoint so that their attitudes may be changed accordingly and they desire also to do what is right.

This process of training must be very simple and very slow. The teacher must lead on carefully and tactfully, always being careful that the pupils modify their conduct, not only because they please her thereby but gradually and principally because, being children of God, they wish to do right for His sake. An occasional little practice cheerfully and well done will do more good than too many practices and resolutions that may easily become burdensome and distasteful. Individual help will be of great benefit where the class is not too large. Some of the pupils will also get help and direction from their parents if they are encouraged to take their problems home for further consultation.

## Scripture Texts

Since the children have learned something about the Bible, they should be encouraged to memorize the simpler Scripture texts and, when occasion presents itself, at any time of the day, the week, or the year, to apply them to particular situations spontaneously.

## The Problems of Everyday Life

The problems are primarily intended to set the pupils thinking about their own actions. Nevertheless, it is much wiser for the teacher not to make the application directly in every case. It is much easier to judge the conduct of somebody else in a particular situation and mete out praise or blame, than it is to judge ourselves. The teacher must be careful to direct attention to the case in hand rather than to the "right answer" which the pupils too often try to read from her face. A great deal of sympathy, skill, and tact are required for this phase of the work. Pupils should be commended for their efforts to solve the problem, even if they do not give the right answer. Under no circumstances should the class be allowed to laugh at mistakes or make exclamations of surprise or reproach. The good should always be stressed in preference to the evil.

## Things to Do

The extra activities suggested furnish assimilative material that is more valuable than may appear at first sight. Learning is a slow process, especially with young children. The extra things to do give them a chance for repetition and review without danger of monotony.

It is especially in activities of this kind, however, that the teacher must be careful not to lose sight of the end for which she is striving. After all, it is not the success of the project itself that counts, nor the variety of materials collected, nor the splendid showing the class makes before visitors. It is, rather, the deepening of the lesson itself and the truths underlying it that has permanent value for the religion class.

It need hardly be pointed out how well these different activities may be fitted into other class periods, depending on their nature. The art work may be done during the art period, the language work during the language period, and so on. The teacher must not, however, make special and strained effort to bring religion into every hour of the day. Rather, all subjects should correlate naturally with one another, and religious thought and principle should permeate all.

## Good Things to Read

If possible the supplementary readers should be placed on a shelf accessible to the pupils at any time. A small table with chairs around it, placed in a corner of the room to suggest a reading atmosphere, would be helpful. Pupils should be free to refer to the books during their spare moments and so have ready for use some of the stories or poems mentioned in their text.

Do not neglect the reading list. The stories and poems listed always have some bearing on the lesson. Other stories and selections may be substituted or added by the pupils. The important thing again is to help along the main thought of the lesson, to enrich and broaden the children's knowledge in reference to the subject in hand.

## Doctrine

The questions referring to the doctrine serve mostly as a review of the truths the children have already learned in the first four grades. The teacher is free to add as many others as she desires. Too much must not be made of formal memorization of definite answers. Principally, children must learn to *live* their religion. Every lesson in the book aims specifically at bringing about this result. It is foolish to believe that memorized lines of doctrine will eventually make good Catholics of pupils. It is the spirit that counts.

Since some instructors may require memory work of the pupils, however, answers to the questions in the text, are added in the manual. The *Baltimore Catechism* may be used as a guide, if desired. It may be well to note here what Father Drinkwater says in this connection in his Introduction to Tahon's *The First Instruction of Children and Beginners,* pages 18 and 19:

"It is asserted that without a fixed form of words, teachers, whether good or bad, will just flounder about vaguely, with no pegs on which to hang their doctrine, so that the children in the end will retain nothing definite at all. This is quite true, of course, but it is not a reason for teaching the answers of the Catechism to young children: it is only a reason why the teacher should often crystallize his teaching into little fixed phrases and sentences which the children will take in and remember. Any tolerable class teacher of young children will soon evolve with them a temporary Catechism of their own, in their own language, and as definite and well-memorized as anybody could wish; but there is all the difference in the world between a living catechesis of that kind, created out of the mental contact of this particular teacher with these particular children, and the process of forcibly feeding children with the official Catechism intended for the grown-up laity; more especially when that process is urged on by regular visits of an outside examiner."

### Poems, Hymns, Quotations, Pictures

The teacher should make it a point to collect suitable poems, hymns, quotations, pictures, and other material for use in her religion class. (See list of special references, p. 193.) A separate envelope or file for the material referring to each lesson would simplify the teacher's daily preparation for another year. Some of the simpler poems should be memorized, others should be read by the teacher for appreciation. Sometimes, as has been mentioned, a poem, hymn, or picture may be used to introduce the day's lesson and arouse new interest and attention. The worth-while selections and songs learned by the class should be frequently repeated. At times some of them may be gathered into an impromptu program for some special feast day. The children will get a great deal of pleasure in taking turns to select the numbers for the program all by themselves. Not all selections, hymns, or pictures need necessarily be of a religious nature. "Religion is life."

The children should be allowed to sing much and often. Preferably such hymns should be selected as are simple, dignified, and devotional. They, too, should be correlated with every subject and used freely at any time that they best serve their purpose. For example, the teacher may have impressed the lesson of fidelity to the pope upon the pupils. They might most fittingly sing, then, "Prayer for the Pope" or some other suitable hymn.

Pictures should also be used freely. At times a picture to be used in introducing a lesson may be put up some days ahead of time so that interest may be aroused and comments and questions exchanged. (See the list of references on page 194; also *Catholic School Journal,* July, 1934, "Pictures in Religious Instruction.")

## Liturgy

The liturgy in its simplest form should go hand in hand with the daily religion lessons. If the Mass has not been studied in the past, the teacher should make it a point to teach the subject as a whole first, before attempting to present individual parts. After the class has a good general knowledge and appreciation of the Mass, it may be considered in its more essential parts. Also the colors of the vestments should be taught and frequently reviewed. Above all, children should be trained to attend Mass with attention and devotion. They should know that they go to Mass to unite themselves with the priest at the altar in offering the Great Sacrifice. They should, therefore, be encouraged to watch the actions of the priest and learn their meaning.

The feasts of the liturgical year should be called to their attention and simple explanations made, when necessary.

The lesson "Saint Thomas More" offers opportunity for a detailed study of the Mass with the class.

A good, simple Mass book or Missal will serve as a splendid guide for a study of the Mass with young children. If the pupil desires to purchase a missal, *Following Christ Through the Mass* (Bruce, Milwaukee), is recommended.

## Creative Work

The teacher should encourage the children to self-expression whenever possible. Plays, stories, poems, drawings, posters, etc., will all become more valuable in proportion to the child's own participation and personal contribution to the activity. Direction will be necessary to some extent, especially at first, but the teacher should always keep in mind that child activity is preferable to teacher activity in working out the assimilative material that is suggested in connection with the lessons.

### Teacher's References

If daily careful preparation is necessary for the teacher in other branches, how much more so in the all-important subject of religion. This manual offers suggestions for the presentation of every lesson in the book. In addition there are references mentioned for the enrichment of the teacher's own knowledge. Naturally the teacher should have a rich background for the subject she is to teach. She should add to or review her own knowledge of Church History as the lessons progress by reading a good text, such as Laux's *Church History,* or *The Life of the Church.*

### Teacher's Notes

In the space left for the teacher's notes questions such as the following should be answered:

Is the length of time suggested for this lesson too long, too short?

What poems, pictures, hymns, stories, etc., have proved most interesting and helpful and where can I find them promptly?

What changes do I desire to make in the work next year?

Is there any criticism of the text? What?

Are there any points I would like to remember for next year?

If necessary an extra blank page may be pasted into the manual for these notes. They are intended as a ready reference and for the improvement for another presentation.

## TO THE REVEREND INSTRUCTOR

The Highway to Heaven Series, of which this book is a part, does not aim to eliminate or minimize the teaching of religious doctrine by the priest. It does, however, offer a new and more interesting approach to the same truths that have always been taught by means of the Catechism alone.

The Reverend Instructor who goes to the classroom once or twice a week, might, if he wishes, follow one of two courses outlined below. In either case the teacher and pupils co-operate with him, so that the best possible results might be obtained from each lesson.

1. The instructor may let the class read and work out the entire lesson prescribed for the week, under the direction of the teacher. He then uses the instruction period to survey the week's work, to assure himself, by questions, that the pupils understand the lesson and all it implies, and then to explain more at length one or more of the doctrinal truths which are suggested at the end of each lesson. Or,

2. He may give his instruction first, and then let the children under the direction of the teacher develop the subject more fully by means of the little exercises and activities suggested in the text. In that case he reviews their work at the beginning of the next instruction and asks questions to assure himself that they have grasped his meaning according to their ability.

### How to Proceed

Take, for example, Lesson 1, "I am the Vine." The teacher has read the story with the children and worked out as many of the assimilative activities as she has found time to include. The instructor first asks a few important questions about the

11

story itself, or better still, about the meaning of the drawings or posters such as are suggested in "Things to Do," which he sees in the classroom. He asks the questions following the lesson and adds others if he desires. He may wish to give his instruction on the Communion of Saints.

Now let us take Lesson 3, "The Birthday of the Church," according to the second method. The instructor first reviews the most important points of his last instructions, possibly looks over the work the class has done during the week, and then introduces the new lesson, "The Descent of the Holy Ghost." Or, he may wish to develop the story itself. The teacher spends the rest of the week reviewing and developing more at length the important thoughts and underlying truths brought out by the instructor.

However, where the Reverend Instructor is entirely in touch with the work of the class there is no reason why he should not, at times, choose the discussion of the life problems or some other phase of the lesson for his own share of the work. He is thereby afforded opportunity to apply his teachings more intimately to the individuals and, incidentally, to know his class better. In any case, it is he who chooses from the lesson the most important doctrinal truths to be taught, leaving the work of review and further development to the classroom teacher.

# RELIGION COURSE FOR GRADE FIVE

*The Plan Outlined*

## Unit I

### How the Church Had Its Beginning

*Time:* September, three weeks.

1. I Am the Vine
   (The Church.
   The Mystical Body of Christ.)
2. Peter, the First Pope
   (The pope, the bishops and priests, the appointed teachers
   of Christ's flock.
   What the pastor is to his flock.)
3. The Birthday of the Church
   (The Holy Ghost, the Third Person of the Blessed Trinity.
   Confirmation and the gifts of the Holy Ghost.)[1]

## Unit II

### The Growth of the Early Church

*Time:* October.

4. St. Stephen, the First Martyr
   (Love your enemies, do good to them that hate you.
   The Spiritual Works of Mercy.)
5. Who Art Thou, Lord?

---

[1]With each lesson the Reverend Instructor will find, in parentheses, one or more correlated topics which may be developed naturally from the story. It is understood, of course, that the work of the year centers around the history of the Church as it is seen through her great leaders. The related topics, while they are reviewed again and again throughout the entire series, do not, in this grade, receive exclusive attention. To be kept in mind primarily, is the Church as the instrument which Christ established to save men, its character as a Mystical Body, and the richness, fullness, and variety of its spiritual life.

13

(What I can do to save souls.
St. Paul, the greatest missionary.)
6. Timothy, Beloved Disciple of St. Paul
   (Holy Scripture.
   Holy Scripture in the Mass.
   The First Commandment.)
7. The Seed of Christianity
   (Faith.
   What I must do to preserve the Faith.)
8. Augustine, Sinner and Saint
   (The mystery of the Holy Trinity.
   Prayer and its qualities.)
9. The Victory of the Cross
   (The sign of the cross.
   The sacramentals.)
10. To Nicaea, to Meet in Council
    (The Nicene Creed.)

## Unit III

### Hidden Heroes of Christ's Church

*Time:* November, first week.

11. Anthony Becomes a Hermit
    (Why we must do penance.
    The punishment due to sin.)
12. Benedict and the Monks
    (Temptation.
    Sin in general.)

## Unit IV

### The Church in the Middle Ages

*Time:* From the second week in November to the
second week in December.

13. Charlemagne Becomes Emperor
    (Obedience to authority, especially civil authority.
    Duties of a good Christian toward his country.)

The corporal works of mercy.)
14. The Holy Land Ruled by Mohammedans
   (Relics of the saints.
   The Fifth Commandment.)
15. God Wills It
   (Christ, our Leader; how we can imitate Him.
   God's Providence.
   The angels.)
16. Louis, King and Saint
   (Mortal sin, the greatest of all evils.)

## Unit V

### Great Popes of the Middle Ages

*Time:* December, second week.

17. Gregory VII
   (Confession.)
18. Innocent III
   (Holy Communion.
   Our duty toward our parents.)

## Unit VI

### Great Saints of the Middle Ages

*Time:* December, third week; January, first
and second weeks.

19. St. Bernard
   (How we can serve God.
   Religious vocations.)
20. The Little Poor Man of Assisi
   (Actions speak louder than words.
   The effect of good and bad example given by Catholics.)
21. The Saint Who Taught the Rosary
   (The Rosary.
   The importance of man's soul.)
22. Well Hast Thou Written of Me, Thomas
   (The Blessed Sacrament.)

## Unit VII

### The Great Revolution

*Time:* January, third and fourth weeks.

23. A Soldier Who Became a Saint
    (Grace, the supernatural life of the soul.)
24. The Council of Trent
    (The sacraments.
    Baptism or Extreme Unction.)

## Unit VIII

### The Church, Mother of Art and Learning

*Time:* February.

25. The Church and Schools
    (The pope and Catholic education.
    Why the Church wants every Catholic child in a Catholic school.)
26. St. John Baptist de la Salle
    (God's gift to man.
    The sacrament of Holy Orders.)
27. Michelangelo
    (Love and care for the house of God.
    Christ's passion and death.)
28. Raphael
    (The Hail Mary.
    I believe in Jesus Christ.)

## Unit IX

### The Church and the Nations

*Time:* March.

30. St. Patrick
    (Faith, hope, and charity.)
31. St. Boniface

(The Good Shepherd.
God's mercy for the sinner.)
32. St. Francis Xavier
(The courage of self-control.
Miracles.)
33. Modern Missionaries
(The Eighth Commandment.)

## Unit X

### The Church as a Teacher

*Time:* April, first half.

34. The Vatican Council
(The authority of the Church.
How the Church got its teachings.)
35. I Am the Immaculate Conception
(Purity.
The Sixth Commandment.)

## Unit XI

### The Church, Mother of All People

*Time:* April, second half.

36. Love Thy Neighbor as Thyself
(The greatest of all commandments.
The Seventh Commandment.)
37. St. Vincent, Father of the Poor
(Thou shalt love thy neighbor as thyself.)

## Unit XII

### The Church, Mother of Saints

*Time:* May, first half.

38. St. Francis of Sales
(Virtue, especially the little virtues.)
39. Woman's work in the Church

(What it means to be a saint.
Devotion to the saints.)

40. The Jesuit Martyrs of North America
(Superstition.
The difference between the use of charms and of blessed articles.)

## Unit XIII

### Other Leaders of the Church

*Time:* May, second half.

41. Saint Thomas More
(The Mass — continued next week.)

42. Daniel O'Connell
(The Mass.
The ideal Catholic follows the Mass intelligently and finds his strength in the Mass and in Holy Communion, an integral part of the Mass.)

43. Frederick Ozanam
(Our duty of gratitude to God.
Count your blessings.)

## Units XIV and XV

### The Church and Peace
### You Are the Branches

*Time:* June.

44. Peace Be with You
(The universality of the Church. We must love men of all nations.)

45. The Church Still Lives
(The continuity of the Church.)

46. Roma!
(Rome, the center of Catholicity.)

## INTRODUCING THE TEXTBOOK TO THE
## CHILDREN

*The Vine and the Branches* is a religion book and should therefore be treated with the reverence and respect due to all religious objects. Before beginning the first lesson, impress the children with this fact. Discuss with them how they might show special care for the book, what they can do to protect it from damage, and so on. The book tells about God, His Church, and His saints. They are our best friends. We should treat them, and all that pertains to them, with special love.

Look at the cover and talk about the symbols. The one in the upper left-hand corner shows the vine and the branches. In the right-hand corner we have the ship of the Church with the Greek letters X P, which stand for the word "Christ," on its sails. (Refer to this symbol again when reading the Introduction to Unit I.) Below is the lily of purity representing the purity of the lives of the Church's saints and on the other side the palm and crown representing the victory (palm) and reward (crown) of the martyrs. The central illustration shows the steep and thorny highway which leads at last to heaven. The Church offers us many helps which bring us safely to the summit.

Find, after reading the title page, the *Nihil obstat* which means "nothing hinders the publication" and the *Imprimatur* of the archbishop. *Imprimatur* means "It may be printed." These two terms show that the book has been examined and approved by ecclesiastical authority, so far as freedom from doctrinal error is concerned.

Explain that the Church is very careful about the religion books that are published, to make sure they do not contain

19

a single word contrary to her teachings. We know that sometimes people write books which teach a false religion. A good
Catholic must always be careful, therefore, that the religious
book he reads has been approved by the Church; that is, that
it has the *Imprimatur* of a bishop or archbishop on it.

Now read and discuss the editor's letter.

# UNIT I

## HOW THE CHURCH HAD ITS BEGINNING

*Time:* Three weeks in September.

### Feasts to Remember

It would be well to have the dates of the following feasts in a conspicuous place on the blackboard or bulletin board. The saints mentioned are principally those whose names will occur in the lessons. It will, therefore, be interesting to the children to have heard something about them before. In fact, the pupils should learn to follow the feasts of the Liturgical Year through the medium of a Catholic Calendar kept in the classroom (or better still in the home, where parents also can use it). While the children are learning about the Church, they should also be taught, through the Liturgy, to live with the Church.

The asterisk indicates names which occur in the children's text. As a help to the teacher, reference is made to the lesson in which the saint's name occurs. The pupils should be encouraged to review the principal events of the story, if it has already been studied. If the lesson is to be read at some future time, however, the pupils should make a short report of the feast from some other source and not from their text. An excellent help is *A Character Calendar* (Bruce, Milwaukee).

September    8    Nativity of the Blessed Virgin Mary
                  (Sing a hymn to Mary.)
            *9    St. Peter Claver
                  (Text, page 204)
            12    Holy Name of Mary
                  (Sing a hymn or read a poem in honor of
                   Mary.)

21

*14  Raising of the Cross
(Text, page 79)

15  Seven Dolors of the Blessed Virgin Mary
("O all you that pass by the way, attend and see, if there be any sorrow like to my sorrow.")

*17  Stigmata of St. Francis
(Text, Lesson 20)

*21  St. Matthew, Apostle and Evangelist

(Have a quotation of St. Matthew's on the blackboard and let the pupils find it in the Bible. The following may be used: "All power is given to Me in heaven and in earth. Going, therefore, teach ye all nations; teaching them to observe all things whatsoever I have commanded you" (xxviii. 18–20).

*26  Jesuit Martyrs of North America
(Text, Lesson 40)

29  St. Michael, Archangel

*The Unit Introduction:*

The introduction suggests the guiding thoughts of the entire unit. It should be read carefully in class and the necessary explanations made by the teacher. In this introduction the Church is compared to a ship of which St. Peter was made the pilot. Have the pupils find a symbol for this thought on the textbook cover. Develop the comparison by such questions as the following:

Who gave us the ship?

Who are in the ship?

When did you get into the ship? (At baptism)

When shall we reach the shore in safety?

Can souls also be shipwrecked? How?

How can we tell from the symbol that the ship belongs to Jesus? (By the sign on the sail)

Unify the three lessons by reading the introduction once more at the conclusion of the entire unit.

## Lesson 1

## I AM THE VINE

*Aim:* Aim to instill into the hearts of the pupils a great love for and pride in the Church. Come back to these thoughts again and again in the course of the week and the year.

*Preparation:* Explain the following words:

*Visible:* that which can be seen by the eyes.

*Invisible:* that which cannot be seen by the eyes.

Have ready, if possible, a good-sized picture (see General References) of Christ Teaching the Multitudes, also pictures of the hierarchy.

Decide on the best way of approaching the lesson. If you feel that you have a more interesting way than that suggested here, be sure to use your own.

Have a few simple stories prepared by the children, showing how Christ taught the people. Example, The Story of the Prodigal Son.

Show a picture of Christ Teaching the Multitudes and let the children talk about it.

Before beginning the reading, create a pleasant but quiet, reverent atmosphere.

*Read Lesson 1*

Now have the pupils read Lesson 1 and talk about it.

If you have a picture or drawing of a grapevine, let the pupils trace the vine and branches to show how all grow from the same root.

Let your own enthusiasm and joy manifest themselves as you go over each sentence.

Learn by means of such questions as follow the lesson, whether the pupils have fully grasped the story. At times these questions may be used to motivate interest before the first reading of the story. For example, you might say: "Read the lesson carefully and see whether you can tell me what the stories which Jesus told, teach us." Vary your approach from week to week. Do not use the same routine all year through.

Usually the story will have to be read a second and perhaps a third time after all explanations have been made and difficulties cleared up.

### Practical Application

The definition for the Church should be explained thoroughly. (Preferably by the Reverend Instructor.) See "To the Reverend Instructor," page 11.

Discuss with the children our membership in the Communion of Saints, showing how we all belong together, just as all the branches of one vine belong together.

Speak of the privilege of being members of the Mystical Body of Christ.

The following comparison may assist you in explaining the Mystical Body of Christ. Explain first the meaning of the words *mystical* and *body. Mystical* comes from mystery, something we cannot fully understand. We shall never be able fully to understand the work of God in man and in His Church. Sometimes we speak of a society or group of people as a body. We say, for example, the student body, the whole body of judges, etc.

Now let us imagine a beautiful chandelier hanging full of clusters of electric bulbs, such as we sometimes see in large churches. Each of these bulbs, taken by itself and disconnected, is practically useless. It cannot give a light, because it has no power of itself. But connected with the electric current, it becomes a shining, brilliant thing, alive with energy, an intimate part of the whole. The bulb is the individual, a member of the Church. In baptism he receives the life of grace. It makes him a member of that group or body, the Church, which receives its life and energy in a mystical manner from Christ. All the electric bulbs in the chandelier, receiving their light from the same current, become intimately related to one another. They form one body. So all who are baptized become members of the same body, of which Christ is the head, the life-giving power.

You can carry the analogy still further. Even after a bulb has been charged with electric power and has given off light in the chandelier, it may gradually become loosened or altogether disconnected, or it may die out. It can no longer give light. So mortal sin acts upon the soul. It takes away the supernatural life, cuts the soul off from the life-giving energy. The soul is supernaturally dead. It is only through confession, or, when confession is not possible, through an act of perfect contrition joined with a desire to receive the sacrament of penance, that the soul is restored to its supernatural life. When an electric bulb is dead, the electrician does not take the time or trouble to repair it. He throws it away. The soul, however, is so precious in the sight of God, that He does not cast it away forever after it has cut itself away from the supernatural life. Through the sacrament of penance it is once more repaired and restored. Also, it can intensify its life; that is, become more and more filled with the power of Christ, through Holy Communion and the other sacraments.

If the question of other religions arises, take a charitable attitude, but make the pupils understand that there can be only *one* true Church, and that is the Catholic Church. There are many good people who think their church is right because, as we shall see later, they have been deceived or because they misunderstand, or are poorly instructed. We must not look down on them or make fun of them. That would show that we are not very kind members of the true Church. Christ, our Head, would surely not approve of that. We should, however, pray for them and ask God to let them find the true Church.

The Church has a wonderful history, which we shall read about from week to week.

*Ask Yourself:*

Do not call for a mere "Yes" or "No" in answer to these questions. The aim is to make religion part of the child's life, to make him *think* and *act* as a Catholic, and not only to talk as such. It is by means of the little discussions and practices that follow each lesson, that the teacher can best accomplish this aim.

*Things to Do:*

This is assimilative material. It serves to impress the lesson on the mind of the child, adds interest, provides purposeful activity, and correlates religion with other subjects.

1. This drawing could be put on the blackboard ahead of time to help illustrate the lesson. Speak again of the Vine and the Branches.

2. Such little suggestions as this may be carried out outside of class time so that the pictures are ready for the class to see.

3. It would be well to devote one entire religion period to stories from the New Testament. They could be used as work in oral English. Some of the lower grade readers and Bible Histories will serve as helps.

4. Talk this over thoroughly. Use the picture on the cover of the textbook as a guide, if necessary. See also Teacher's References.

5. This offers opportunity to renew interest in the prayers of the Mass and to give the children a better understanding of them. The pupils should be reminded that they are taking part in the Sacrifice of the Mass, as indicated so often in the prayers, in such words as the following: "who offer up to Thee this sacrifice of praise for themselves and theirs."

6. A few words about Cardinal Newman begging God to help him find the truth, will give this activity a closer connection with the lesson.

7. Any Scripture text that is to be memorized by the children must be well explained. It is useless to burden the memory with meaningless words. The texts show that the branches are fed by the Vine.

*Can You Answer These Questions?*

This is a review of the doctrine following naturally from the lesson. If the instructor desires, the words may be memorized according to any Catechism; if not, aim at a thorough understanding and simple statement of the truth.

In connection with this and the two following lessons, the names of the hierarchy should be learned; that is, the name of the pope and also the cardinal or archbishop, the bishop, the pastor and assistant priests in direct connection with the parish. An interesting project could be worked out in pictures in this connection.

1. God created us to know Him, to love Him, and to serve Him in this world, and to be happy with Him forever in the next.

2. In order to go to heaven we must do all that God and His Church command us to do.

3. He has left us His Church to teach and guide us.

4. Jesus Christ founded the Church.

5. Text, page 4.

6. Christ founded the Church to teach, govern, sanctify, and save all men.

7. He founded the Church for everybody.

8. No, many people do not belong to the Church.

9. Text, page 5.

10. Text, page 5.

11. We should help the members of the Church Militant by praying for them, by doing acts of kindness for them, by keeping them from sin and showing them the right way by our good example.

12. We should help the Church Suffering by praying for them, gaining indulgences for them, doing good works for them.

13. November 1.

14. November 2.

15. The souls in purgatory are the souls of those who died in venial sin and cannot go to heaven until they are purified from all temporal punishment due to sin.

16. By saying indulgenced prayers, performing good works, learning our catechism. (See Reference on page 28.)

17. An indulgence is the remission, in whole or in part, of the temporal punishment due to sin.

*Teacher's References:*

*The Holy Bible,* John xv.

*Catholic School Journal,* October, 1933. Editorial on Indulgence for those devoted to teaching or learning catechism.

*Catholic Action Series,* Book III, "The Church, The Mystical Body of Christ," pages 18–21.

*Teacher's Notes:*

## Lesson 2

## PETER, THE FIRST POPE

*Aim:* This lesson aims to show how Peter was appointed the first pope and what great power he received to rule as visible head of the Church.

*Preparation:* Have a picture of St. Peter receiving the keys, of the Vatican, and of St. Peter's in Rome. Have simple clippings pertaining to the pope posted on the bulletin board and let the pupils add others from day to day. A picture of Pope Pius XI should bear the words: "He takes the place of St. Peter today."

Teach the "Hymn for the Pope" (Textbook, p. 13) and have the class sing it frequently during the year, especially during the Church Unity Octave, January 17 to 25.

As an approach to the lesson ask questions such as the following:

What is the Church?

Do you belong to the Church?

How can you prove that you belong to the Church? (Use definition of the Church.)

Who rules the Church?

Today we shall hear how Peter was made the first pope by Jesus Christ Himself.

*Read Lesson 2*

Talk about the lesson and about the picture on page 9.

Did Jesus really give Peter keys? The keys are only used as a sign or symbol of the power given to Peter.

*Practical Application*

Call attention to the number of popes that have ruled the Church since the time of Peter. Many of the early popes were martyrs.

Loyalty to and love for the Holy Father can be cultivated in a number of ways: by frequent and loving reference to him in the classroom, by prayer for him and his intentions, by teaching the hymn for the pope and singing it frequently, and especially by interesting the pupils in newspaper and magazine articles referring to him and to his activities and pronouncements in behalf of the Church. Care must be taken, of course, to keep within the capacity of the children. There is no reason, however, why they should not hear something about current affairs of the Church in a simple, informal way. This should be the spirit throughout: as members of the Mystical Body of Christ, to live in intimate union with and feel keenly for all members of the Church, especially for its visible head, the pope. We are all branches of the same vine; we should feel for one another, love one another and pray for one another, especially for those who rule and guide us. Encourage the children to read and bring items about the Holy Father from their little school papers and magazines.

Make use of the prayer for the pope to stimulate interest in the prayers said for different intentions during the Mass. The prayer is that found in the missal. It will need to be simplified for the children.

*Things to Do:*

1. Such stories as this may be assigned to individuals ahead of time so that they are prepared in time for the religion period or, if there are more books on hand, they may be read for silent reading by the entire class. Vary the assignment from time to time, and gradually give the more timid pupils a chance also to come out and relate what they have read. In doing this, you are giving valuable character training at the same time that you are teaching religion.

2. Have the children look for the symbol, the keys of St. Peter, in church. They are the symbol of the authority of the Church given by Christ Himself to St. Peter.

3. This assignment may be varied. Cut-out work, clay modeling, and carving may all be called into play for the purpose. Be sure, however, that the pupils associate the meaning of St. Peter's keys with their work, whatever form it takes.

4. See map on page 78. A simple outline map of Palestine might be made by the children and the various places added

from time to time, or a hectographed outline map may be provided for each child and the important places inserted.

5. A repetition of the story in connection with the drawing is, of course, the important thing. Encourage the pupils to take their work home and tell the story to their parents.

6. The bishop's staff is called a crosier. Write the word on the blackboard and explain that it comes from the word "cross." Have the children point out the similarity between the two words.

7. Pope Pius XI is at the head of the Church today (1935).

8. The "Hymn for the Pope" should preferably be taught according to the melody by H. G. Ganss. It is published in a leaflet for the Church Unity Octave by the Lamp Publishing Co., Garrison, N. Y., and sells 10 copies for 25 cents, or 100 copies for $1.

9. Naturally the children should be encouraged throughout the year to notice such and similar articles.

10. It would be well to have a few children tell the class some interesting facts about the Vatican.

11. Scripture texts such as this should be put to frequent use throughout the year. They must be memorized word for word.

If you have a stamping outfit from the Creative Education Co. (see General References) you can use it to good advantage here. It contains a picture of the pope, also of St. Peter and the Church.

## Can You Answer These Questions?

1. Jesus could see and know all things because He is God.

2. Jesus Christ is the invisible head of the Church.

3. The pope is the visible head of the Church.

4. The people belonging to the Church and their priests are the lambs and sheep of the flock.

5. By these words Christ promised to St. Peter, the head of the Church, the supreme power of teaching, governing, and sanctifying the members of the Church.

6. The enemies of the Church cannot destroy her. "And the gates of hell shall not prevail against it."

The Hymn for the Pope will require some explanations.

*Teacher's References:*

*The Holy Bible,* Matt. xvi. 13–20; John xxi.

*Catholic Action Series,* Book I, "The Pope," pages 22–25.

*Teacher's Notes:*

## Lesson 3

*Aim:* To learn about the birthday of the Church and that, as true members of that Church we must not only *know* the truths she teaches but also *live* them, just as the first Christians did, who were converted by the Apostles.

*Preparation:* Read over the entire lesson and make your plans for the week. Gather whatever pictures you can that have a bearing on the lesson, beginning with the Ascension of Christ. Before reading the lesson, have the children read or tell the story of the Ascension and dwell especially on the promise of Christ to send the Holy Ghost.

*Read Lesson 3*

Answer the questions. Talk over the lesson paragraph by paragraph. The Apostles were afraid to show themselves. They remained behind locked doors. What a great change came over them after they had received the Holy Ghost. They unlocked the doors and even went out to preach.

Once the converted people knew what to do, they lived beautiful, simple lives. That proved more than anything else that they believed all that the Apostles told them.

*Practical Application*

Discuss the cases given. They give you an excellent chance to bring home to the pupils the idea that, to be Christians in the best sense of the word, they must *live* their religion as the early Christians did. They are themselves responsible to God for their conduct. A good Catholic child should not need a watchman to see that he does the right thing. He knows what is right, and he knows that God sees him. That should be enough for him. Give time for quiet thought.

*Things to Do:*

1. Talk also about the intervening time between the Ascension and the coming of the Holy Ghost, showing how the Apostles spent their time, what they might have talked about, etc.

2. Explain that the Feast of Pentecost depends upon the date on which Easter occurs.

3. Unless there is a map available, there is no need to look further for these places.

4. Let the story begin with the early morning on Pentecost Day, as told by someone who heard the rumbling noise and ran to see what had happened.

5. The dove may also be used as a motif for a drawing pattern.

6. *Wisdom* makes us like the things of God and act so that we give Him honor and glory.

*Understanding* helps us to know more clearly the mysteries of our faith.

*Counsel* warns us against the devil and the dangers to our soul.

*Fortitude* strengthens us to do the will of God in all things.

*Knowledge* helps us to discover the will of God in all things.

*Piety* helps us to love God as a Father and obey Him because we love Him.

*Fear* of the Lord fills us with a dread for sin.

7. Explain the meaning of *divers* — different kinds. Encourage the children, when repeating the story, to use these words exactly as they occur in the text.

8. Use this occasion to review the prayer to the Holy Ghost which the children ordinarily say, especially for confession. Help them acquire a more intimate knowledge of the prayers commonly used so that prayer may become for them more and more a thing of the heart and less a thing of the lips.

9. "King Robert of Sicily" is one of Longfellow's well-known poems.

If the children know a hymn to the Holy Ghost, let them sing it.

### Can You Answer These Questions?

1. The Holy Ghost is the third Person of the Blessed Trinity.

2. God the Father is the first Person of the Blessed Trinity.

3. Jesus Christ is the second Person of the Blessed Trinity.

4. The Blessed Trinity is one God in three Divine Persons.

5. We cannot fully understand how the three Divine Persons can be one and the same God because it is a mystery.

6. A mystery is a truth which we cannot fully understand.

7. The third decade, glorious mystery.

8. We should pray to the Holy Ghost especially when we need light to know the right thing to do or to say. For example, before we examine our conscience at confession.

9. We should pray to the Holy Ghost because He is the third Person of the Blessed Trinity who is the Spirit of Love and because He enlightens our minds and helps us to know what is right.

10. Baptism, Penance, and in a special manner Confirmation and Holy Orders.

11. Baptism is the sacrament which takes away original sin from our souls, makes us Christians, children of God, and heirs of heaven.

12. Confirmation is the sacrament through which we receive the Holy Ghost to make us strong and perfect Christians and soldiers of Christ.

13. We know what God wants us to do from the commandments and from the Catholic Church through which God speaks to us.

*Return to Introduction to This Unit:*

As a final summary or clinching or organization of this unit, return to its introductory statement and read it again and discuss in the light of all the material of the unit.

*Teacher's References:*

*The Holy Bible,* Acts ii.

*Catholic Action Series,* Book I, "The Sacrament of Baptism," pages 210–219; "Confirmation," pages 220–227.

*The Life of the Church,* "The Preaching of the Twelve and the Infant Church," pages 69–75.

*Teacher's Notes:*

# UNIT II

# THE GROWTH OF THE EARLY CHURCH

*Time:* October, four weeks.

### Feasts to Remember

| | | |
|---|---|---|
| October | 2 | Guardian Angel |
| | *3 | St. Therese, The Little Flower |
| | | (Text, page 254) |
| | *4 | St. Francis of Assisi |
| | | (Give a little play in honor of St. Francis. See *Catholic School Journal,* March, 1934.) |
| | *7 | Most Holy Rosary |
| | | (Lesson 21) |
| | *15 | St. Teresa of Avila |
| | | (Text, page 255) |
| | 18 | St. Luke, the Evangelist |
| | | (Wrote one of the Gospels and the Acts of the Apostles. Have the pupils find both in the Bible.) |
| | 24 | St. Raphael, the Archangel |
| | | (Recall the story of Tobias.) |
| | 29 | SS. Simon and Jude, Apostles |
| | | (Have the pupils find where these two Apostles went to spread the faith and how they died.) |

Last Sunday in October, Feast of Christ the King.

## *The Unit Introduction:*

The introduction to each unit gives the pupils a general view of the unit as a whole. Make the most of it by assuring yourself that the pupils know what they should expect and how it is linked with the past.

37

Two expressions will probably need some explanation: "The blood of martyrs is the seed of Christianity" and "the price Christ's followers had to pay before the victory was won." A few practical examples may help: We plant a tiny apple seed. It seems as though it had to die. It was necessary for the seed to be buried before a tree could develop. But from it a tree comes, and later we get a whole crop of fruit from the tree.

If we want food, we have to pay a price for it. If we want learning, the price we have to pay is hard study. If we want a healthy body, the price is careful observance of the rules of health. Many of Christ's followers had to give their lives to keep the Faith. The price of the great victory of Christianity was the lives of thousands of Christians.

Come back at the end of the unit and verify by examples from the book what price the saints mentioned in the text had to pay for their faith.

### Lesson 4

*Aim:* To learn from the story of St. Stephen how the Jews hated the Christians and what a Christlike life the early members of the Church lived.

*Preparation:* Have on hand a picture of the crucifixion. Under it may be written such words as, "He forgave His enemies" or "Father, forgive them . . . ."

In preparation for the lesson explain the attitude of the Jews toward the Christians. The Jews had rejected Christ and had done everything in their power to wipe out his memory. Among them were some who honestly believed they were right in persecuting the Christians.

### Read Lesson 4

Explain any word[1] or passage that is not clear.

Point out that punishment by crucifixion was meant for only the lowest criminals. People could not bear the sight of a cross.

---

[1]Thorndike's *Century Junior Dictionary* should be helpful here and throughout the text.

Naturally some of them could not see how anyone who died on a cross should be looked upon as God.

Dwell especially on St. Stephen's forgiveness of his enemies in imitation of Christ, his leader.

*What Would You Do?*

These problems apply the lesson to the daily life of the child.

We partake of the life of the Vine, which is Christ. We ought to carry out in our conduct, as St. Stephen did, that Christlife, of which we partake.

Point out that it is by practicing patience in little things that we become stronger for the really big and hard things. Again, give the pupils a chance to talk about these and similar situations and to do a little thinking of their own. Often by letting pupils express themselves, the teacher will find that many are already imbued with the spirit of retaliation and revenge. Above all, she must not express surprise or be in any way shocked at these false conceptions of justice. She must aim, by sympathetic understanding, to lead the pupils on gradually to the practice of truly Christian principles. She must remember, too, that a mere statement of the truths may not be sufficient to convince a child. On the other hand, she must be careful not to put pupils under the impression that one must be a weakling in order to be forgiving or that one must relinquish all rights to justice in order to be virtuous.

Your readers offer many little stories illustrating the point that it takes more than usual bravery to control oneself under difficult circumstances. Give the pupils the pleasure of looking for such stories themselves. Similarly, if you can be reasonably sure that the pupils can find a required picture, let them bring it, in place of doing so yourself; or at least let them post it on the bulletin board and talk about it to the class. In other words, do not do for the pupils the simple tasks which they can do for themselves and which they would enjoy doing.

*Things to Do:*

1. Form in the pupils the habit of living in the spirit of the

Church. Have them take notice of the more important feasts and watch day by day for the color of the vestments the priest wears at Mass. Be sure to have a Catholic calendar in your classroom.

3. The story of St. John Gualbert can be found in Butler's *Lives of the Saints,* July 12.

6. Here is an opportunity to review the words and meaning of the Our Father. Call the children's attention to the fact that we ask God to forgive us *as we* forgive those who have wronged us.

7. (1) To warn sinners,
    (2) To instruct the ignorant,
    (3) To counsel the doubting,
    (4) To comfort the sorrowing,
    (5) To bear wrongs patiently,
    (6) To forgive wrongs,
    (7) To pray for the living and the dead.

8. Esau forgave Jacob. Joseph forgave his brethren.

*Can You Answer These Questions?*

1. We should love our enemies because Christ commands us to do so.

2. By praying for them, showing that we have no hard feelings against them, doing good to them, etc.

3. Against the Fifth Commandment.

4. Thou shalt not kill.

5. It forbids us to harm ourselves or others in body or soul.

6. We must take reasonable care to keep our bodies clean and healthy.

7. We must take care of our own bodies because they are the gift of God and temples of the Holy Spirit. (Explain more fully.)

Activities referring to health and the care of our bodies can be easily correlated with this lesson. The teacher should be on the alert for opportunities to make use of actual situations in the classroom. If she notices, for example, that children come to school with wet shoes and stockings through their own carelessness she may point out that proper care of our health is not a matter of choice but of duty.

*Teacher's References:*

*The Holy Bible,* Acts vi, vii.

*Church History,* St. Stephen, the Proto Martyr, page 10.

*Journal of Religious Instruction,* "Does Your Catholic Calendar Do Its Full Share of Work?", December, 1933.

*Catholic Action Series,* Book II, Chap. XXI.

*Teacher's Notes:*

## Lesson 5

*Aim:* To learn how the Church continued the work of Christ through the Apostles and especially through St. Paul, the great Apostle of the Gentiles.

*Preparation:* If there is time, assign to individual members of the class the lives of the Apostles to be related in short to the class.

Words that may need explanation: *zeal; Christian communities; forty stripes save one; thrice; perils.*

The Jews had killed Christ and they had killed Stephen. They were determined to put an end to all the Christians. No one could help them more than the zealous young man Saul. And he was most eager to do his share. We shall hear his story in today's lesson.

### *Read Lesson 5*

Go over the lesson paragraph by paragraph. Explain particularly St. Paul's quoted words: "Of the Jews five times did I receive forty stripes, save one," etc. Review the lesson several times in order to make sure that the pupils get the full significance of the burning zeal and tremendous missionary labors of St. Paul.

### *Practical Application*

There are still many people to convert. People who live near us and people in other lands. What are we willing to do to help them become members of the true Church, branches of the great Vine?

Have on hand sample copies of the *Little Missionary,* the *Field Afar,* the *Indian Sentinel,* and other mission magazines.

Say a prayer for the missions with the class. Encourage the children to pray for the conversion of pagans of their own accord. As members of the Communion of Saints they should learn to make the cause of the Church their own. Your own attitude and zeal will be quickly reflected by the class in this matter.

*Things to Do:*

1. Let the children suggest their own plans.

2. This work is interesting and at the same time easy enough for all to do. It need not be finished in a hurry.

3. Other mission magazines should be added.

4. Recall that these journeys were made largely on foot and by ship.

5. June 29. Red vestment, because they were both martyrs.

6. January 25.

7. To Timothy, the Romans, the Colossians, the Corinthians, the Thessalonians, the Philippians, the Ephesians, etc.

8. See Teacher's References.

9. "Lord, what wilt Thou have me do?"

10. Make use of this opportunity to correlate with the history lesson.

11. Give the children the pleasure of collecting and posting these pictures themselves.

12. St. Paul holds a sword, indicating the manner of his martyrdom.

13. Have these lives related to the class. This may be done during the oral English period.

14. St. John the Evangelist.

15. Feasts of the Apostles — including St. Matthias, who took the place of Judas, and St. Paul who was not among the original twelve.

Watch for these feasts as they occur.

| February | 24, | St. Matthias |
|----------|-----|--------------|
| May | 1, | SS. Philip and James |
| June | 11, | St. Barnabas |
| June | 29, | SS. Peter and Paul |
| July | 25, | St. James |
| August | 24, | St. Bartholomew |
| September | 21, | St. Matthew |
| October | 29, | SS. Simon and Jude |
| November | 30, | St. Andrew |
| December | 21, | St. Thomas |

16. Make sure that the text is well understood.

*Can You Answer These Questions?*
1. Because Christ told them to go out and teach all nations.
2. Christ Himself, who is God, gave them the right.
3. The Apostles' Creed.
4. The Holy Bible.
5. Eating only one full meal a day.
6. Because the Church commands them to fast at certain times as a penance for their sins.
7. All over twenty-one and under sixty years of age.
8. Perform many little acts of self-denial. (Examples)

St. Paul spent his life spreading the faith. The prayer by which we profess our own belief in all that the Church teaches is the Apostles' Creed. Review the Creed and, if necessary, explain, in short, the individual articles.

*Teacher's References:*

*The Holy Bible,* Acts x.

*A Book of Religion for Elementary Schools:* "Society for the Propagation of the Faith" and "Association of the Holy Childhood," pages 295–297.

*Church History,* "The Conversion of St. Paul," page 11.

*The Life of the Church,* "The Preaching of St. Paul," pages 75–83.

*Teacher's Notes:*

## Lesson 6

*Aim:* To learn how St. Timothy became a disciple of St. Paul and what he did for the early Church.

*Preparation:* Approach the new lesson by recalling that St. Paul formed new communities wherever he went. That means that he had to train good men to be the shepherds of the new flocks. The Holy Bible tells us an interesting story about a young man who became a companion of St. Paul and later a bishop. We shall read that story today.

### Read Lesson 6

Explain that the pagans adored false gods and sometimes sacrificed also to men whom they thought to be gods. Did the Apostles allow them to offer sacrifice to them? Why not?

Have one or more copies of the Holy Bible in the room for the children to use. Also have copies of the New Testament on hand, to show the various forms under which the Scripture may be published. Refer also to page 148 of the text.

Locate Lystra on the map of St. Paul's Journeys.

*Things to Do:*

1. Speak here of the reverence we should have for the word of God.

At Mass we rise when the priest reads the Gospel. See whether you can form in the children the habit of listening reverently and attentively to the Gospel read on Sundays, and also to the sermon which usually follows. It may be necessary to prepare the Gospel with them to some extent at first. The word of God, they should be told, should always be listened to with great reverence, no matter how often we hear the same story read. As we grow older, we shall understand it better and find that there are always new thoughts for us to learn.

2. Show the New Testament in a separate binding. Show also that one Bible may look altogether different from another as to binding, print, pictures, etc., but let them see that the words are exactly the same.

3. "Paul an apostle of Jesus Christ, according to the commandment of God our Saviour, and of Christ Jesus our hope.

"To Timothy, his beloved son in faith — Grace, mercy, and peace from God the Father, and from Christ Jesus our Lord."

Find also the quotation on page 33 of the text (II Tim. iv. 6–8).

4. Many Catholics do not know a Catholic Bible from a non-Catholic one. Review this little lesson on the Bible occasionally until you are sure that the children recognize a book that has the approval of the hierarchy and know just how much that implies. It does not imply that the work itself is scholarly or of literary value. It means only that the book is free from all error as far as religious teaching is concerned.

5. In his letter to Timothy, St. Paul says (I Tim. iv. 13): "Till I come, attend unto reading, to exhortation, and to doctrine." Have the children look for this text.

6. St. Timothy, January 24.

7. Correlate with written language work. Let the children use a salutation similar to that of St. Paul.

8. Allow the children to use their own initiative. If necessary, direct them to certain details in the story but on the whole let them use their own ideas.

*Can You Answer These Questions?*

1. The Holy Bible is the book which contains the inspired word of God.

2. Into two main parts, the Old Testament and the New Testament.

3. Seventy-two books.

4. The Old Testament contains the story of the Jewish nation from the Creation to the birth of Christ. The New Testament contains the history of Christ's life and death in the four gospels of Matthew, Mark, Luke, and John, the Acts of the Apostles, and the other writings of the Apostles.

5. Because sacrifice may be offered to God alone.

6. The First Commandment.

7. Sins against faith, hope, charity.

8. This commandment does not forbid us to honor the saints.

9. We are not allowed to pray to crucifixes or to images and relics of the saints, for they have no life nor power to help us, nor sense to hear us. We sometimes kneel before an image of the person to whom we are praying.

10. Yes, the saints can hear us because they are with God who makes our prayers known to them.

Recall that a great many prayers said at Mass are taken from Holy Scripture. A better understanding of Holy Scripture therefore means a better understanding of Holy Mass.

*Teacher's References:*

*Church History,* "St. Paul's Second Great Mission Tour," page 20.

Laux, *Introduction to the Bible,* Part I.

*A Book of Religion for Elementary Schools,* "The Bible or Sacred Scripture," page 290.

*Catholic School Journal:* "The Book of Books," October, 1933.

*Teacher's Notes:*

## Lesson 7

*Aim:* To learn how the blood of the martyrs became the seed of Christianity and thereby to cultivate a deep love for the Catholic Church and a strong determination never to part with it.

*Preparation:* Have as many pictures as possible of martyrs, the catacombs, the Roman circus, etc., also stories of the early martyrs. Note the aim for this week and keep it well in mind.

We have already learned what it means to "pay the price" for something we need or want. We shall see in our today's story what price the early Christians were willing to pay to keep their faith and so to remain attached to the true Vine.

**Read Lesson 7**

Do not elaborate so much on the terrible torments suffered by the martyrs, but dwell largely on their steadfastness, their love of God, and their determination to die rather than to lose the faith. Point out, then, how little it takes sometimes to make people unfaithful to God and their religion. A little money, a bit of pleasure is enough to make some people turn their backs on God.

The children will, of course, all attest their willingness to give their lives for their faith. They prove their strength, however, by the *little* things they are willing to do or give up for God each day. Enumerate with them the many little sacrifices they can make each day in order to prove their willingness to live according to their Christian faith.

**Practical Application**

Say a little prayer of thanks with the children for the gift of faith, but encourage them often to express their gratitude to God of their own accord without waiting for someone to remind them.

**Things to Do:**

1. The *Religion in Life Curriculum,* which outlines the entire Highway to Heaven Series, gives a list of the saints whose stories are to be found in Catholic readers.

2. Use the stories from the readers as a guide.

4. This little exercise is just an opportunity to test out the pupils' imaginative powers. If some of the letters are good, have them read to the class.

5. Tell or read to the class something about these two Apostles.

6. See also map on page 30.

7. This should bring to light a great deal of interesting material.

8. Throughout the lessons in the book, bring out the beautiful character traits of the great saints and leaders. Such an exercise is very helpful in training for character.

9. Such a booklet, if the class wishes to make one, should be worked on over a long period of time. Since the work of this year centers around the history of the Church as exemplified largely in the lives of the great heroes who lived and worked in the various periods, it seems most appropriate to make a special study of the lives of the saints and to note their contribution to the Church's history.

A secondary aim in making a book of this kind, is to teach the children purposeful activity for their leisure moments — to cultivate a hobby. In that case the book could be started well on its way in school and later continued at home according to the interest of the pupil. A loose-leaf notebook or scrapbook would serve the purpose best. Perhaps just a character trait or a worth-while saying or some interesting incident could be noted about each saint, and a picture added if possible. There are interesting variations. Let the pupils plan for themselves.

## Can You Answer These Questions?

1. Faith is that gift of God by which we accept all that the Church teaches because we know that she cannot teach what is not true.

2. Have the children tell the different ways in which they can show their faith and why they show their faith by a particular action, such as keeping from sin, praying, genuflecting, etc.

3. In baptism.

4. The gifts of hope and charity.

5. We sin against faith by
   a) Doubting in matters of faith,
   b) Not believing everything that the Church teaches.

       *c*) Not believing at all,

       *d*) Giving up our faith altogether.

6. We sin against hope

       *a*) By not hoping at all (despair),

       *b*) By hoping too much (presumption).

7. We sin against love of God by not keeping His commandments.

8. Review whatever acts the children know.

9. Baptism is a sacrament which cleanses the soul from original sin, makes us Christians, children of God, and heirs of heaven.

10. It also takes away all sins committed before baptism and all temporal and eternal punishment due to sin.

11. In case of necessity anyone who has the use of reason may baptize.

15. To believe firmly in the teachings of the Catholic Church; to avoid evil; to lead a truly Christian life.

17. They must take care that the child is brought up in the Catholic Faith in case the parents neglect their duty or die.

*Teacher's References:*

*Church History*, "The Age of Martyrs," pages 48–82.

*Catholic Action Series*, Book II, "The Worship of God," pages 230–246.

*The Life of the Church*, "Church and State," "Persecutions," pages 100–111.

*Teacher's Notes:*

### Lesson 8

*Aim:* To learn about the great work of St. Augustine for the Church and to understand what the titles "Father of the Church" and "Doctor of the Church" mean.

*Preparation:* If you can take the time, have individual pupils prepare short sketches of the lives of some of the Fathers and Doctors of the Church mentioned in this lesson. Obtain pictures of them, if possible, and have the pupils find the date of their feasts. Recall them again to mind as the feasts occur.

Ask the following question in preparation for the new lesson: "What stories from the life of Christ show that He loved sinners?" (Good Shepherd, Prodigal Son, Mary Magdalen, Good Thief)

Ever since the time of Christ, the Church, too, has received sinners into her arms just as the Good Shepherd brought back the lost sheep. Today we shall hear about one of these sinners who became a shining light in the Church.

*Read Lesson 8*

Stress the faith, hope, and perseverance of St. Monica in her prayer for St. Augustine.

This is an excellent opportunity to bring home to the children more intimately the necessity of that faith of which we spoke in the last lesson. The mind of man is so small in comparison with that of God, that it would be very, very difficult indeed, to understand such mysteries of the faith as the Blessed Trinity. In fact, he cannot do it. It is truly a mystery.

Explain what is meant by "a strong Christian Community." It means that at Augustine's death there was a fervent group of Christians gathered together in one place, forming something like a parish or diocesan group.

Have the children find the Feast of St. Monica and tell something about her life.

Be sure to dramatize the incident on the seashore. It will help to deepen the impression of man's insignificance in comparison with God.

*Can You Answer These Questions?*

1. We were created to know, love, and serve God in this world and to be happy with Him forever in heaven.

2. "Our hearts are restless until they rest in Thee, O Lord."

3. Because the little mind of man can never grasp the great mind of God.

4. The Glory be to the Father, and the sign of the cross.

5. Under God, to his mother.

6. She prayed for his conversion for twenty years.

7. Prayer is the lifting up of the mind and heart to God. (It is not merely repeating words.)

8. Prayer is necessary to save our soul. Through prayer we receive the graces necessary to carry on our daily tasks according to the will of God.

9. The Our Father, because Christ Himself taught it.

11. For our parents, brothers and sisters, relatives, friends, the poor souls, the pope, the Church, sinners, etc.

12. *a)* Every morning and evening,

*b*) Before and after meals,

*c*) On Sundays and holydays,

*d*) In times of sickness, necessity, temptation.

13. We should pray with devotion, with humility, with confidence, with resignation, and with perseverance.

Give practical examples of each of the above qualities of prayer.

14. We should remember that we are talking to God and behave accordingly.

*Teacher's References:*

*The Holy Bible*, Luke xviii. 10.

*Church History*, "St. Augustine, the Doctor of Grace," pages 138–151.

*Catholic Action Series*, Book I, "Prayer," pages 291–299.

*The Life of the Church*, "St. Augustine," pages 146–150.

*Teacher's Notes:*

## Lesson 9

*Aim:* To learn how the Church was finally triumphant over paganism through the victory of Constantine.

*Preparation:* Call to mind that it was not only the Emperor Nero who persecuted the Christians, but most of the Roman emperors who ruled the great empire for three hundred years. How many Christians might have been killed in that time? Thousands and hundreds of thousands. They did not dare to show themselves openly as Christians. For their religious services they crept way down under the earth, into the catacombs. But in spite of all persecution, the time came when the Christians could come out from under the earth and practice their religion openly. Today we shall hear what happened to bring about that change.

*Read Lesson 9*

Try to give the children some conception of the joy that must have come over the Christians, especially those of Rome, when at last they were free to worship the true God openly.

The pagans hated the cross. It was a sign of great shame. Only slaves and the lowest criminals were nailed to the cross. Men shuddered and turned away at the very sight of it. Now it is a sign of honor among Christians. Recall the various occasions during the day when we use the sign of the cross. We should make the sign of the cross immediately on awakening. We begin and end our prayers with the sign of the cross. The priest begins the Mass, the greatest act of Christian worship, with the sign of the cross. In fact, he uses the sign of the cross more than thirty times during the Mass.

Have the pupils take special notice of the sign of the cross made by the priest during Mass.

### Practical Application

It would be well to have the different shapes of crosses suggested at the end of the lesson cut out and mounted on the bulletin board or drawn on the blackboard.

Have a good-sized crucifix or the picture of the crucifixion on hand.

Keep well in mind the aim of this week's activities. Gather as much material as you can, pertaining to the lesson. Especially enrich your own store of knowledge and devotion in all that pertains to the cross. For that purpose read with prayerful devotion, Book II, Chapter XII, of *The Following of Christ*.

The suggested booklet makes a very interesting and easy activity. For some of the shapes of crosses see Brother Eugene in the references below, or the *Catholic School Journal*.

### Things to Do:

1 and 2. Be sure to call for the story in connection with the drawing.

3. The children should by this means be made aware of the presence or absence of the crucifix especially in their homes.

4. The aim of this little exercise is to impress more deeply upon the children the futility of any earthly power to overcome Christianity.

5. The Finding of the Holy Cross, May 3, and the Exaltation of the Holy Cross, September 14.

See the *St. Andrew Daily Missal* for further explanation of these feasts. Note especially the Communion Verse which is simple enough for the children to understand.

6. I N R I are the initials for the Latin words meaning "Jesus of Nazareth, King of the Jews."

7. From Passion Sunday to Holy Thursday, in order to give the faithful a more intimate share in the sorrow of the Church and also in memory of Jesus hiding Himself from His enemies.

*Can You Answer These Questions?*

1. We make the sign of the cross to make known our faith in Christ and His Church.

2. The mystery of the Holy Trinity.

3. On rising, before and after prayer, in temptation, on taking Holy Water, etc.

4. On Good Friday in memory of Christ's death on the cross.

5. A sacramental is anything set apart or blessed by the Church to awaken good thoughts and to increase devotion and through these movements of the heart to remit venial sin.

6. Holy water, benediction, blessed candles, blessed medals.

7. (*a*) The sacraments were instituted by Jesus Christ and the sacramentals by the Church.

(*b*) The sacraments give grace of themselves when we place nothing in the way; the sacramentals awaken in us pious thoughts by means of which we may obtain grace.

*Teacher's References:*

*Church History,* "The Triumph of the Cross," pages 75–77.

*A Book of Religion for Elementary Schools,* "Crosses" (pictures of various kinds) page 300.

*The Life of the Church,* "Church and State, The End of the Roman World," pages 150–159.

*Catholic Encyclopedia,* "The Sign of the Cross."

*Teacher's Notes:*

### Lesson 10

*Aim:* To learn how the Church exercises the power given her by Jesus Christ especially at the time of a General Council.

*Preparation:*

At times the name *Ecumenical Council* is used in place of General Council. Have the name on the blackboard so that the children can see it for themselves.

This lesson requires special care and preparation. Do not go into further details, but try to make clear the points mentioned in the lesson.

The Council of Nicaea or Nice (pronounced like "niece") was the first General Council held. The Council of Jerusalem in A.D. 49 is not counted as a General Council.

Perhaps the following example will help you explain the necessity of such meetings of the most learned men of the Church:

When there were only a few automobiles in the whole United States, there was no need for any traffic laws, traffic cops, etc. Why? Today it is altogether different. Why are there so many traffic laws to obey now and why is so much care taken that these laws are obeyed? What would happen if no one kept these laws even for one day? It is the same with the Church. As long as there were only a few Christians and the Apostles were still with them to tell them what they had to believe and do, there was little need to make laws. But when Christianity spread all over the world and times changed, it became necessary to make laws and to explain what the Church teaches, so that all, even those who lived far, far away, might know exactly what to believe and do in order to be saved.

*Read Lesson 10*

Note that it is the pope who calls a General Council.

The Nicene Creed does not teach anything that Christ did not teach, but defines more clearly the same truths the Church has always taught.

*Practical Application*

Have the children take notice of the Creed when it is said at Mass. Encourage them to say it along with the priest. Remind them that they are members of the Mystical Body of Christ and that they join with thousands of others in professing their faith, the same faith that the bishops and priests professed at Nicaea more than 1,600 years ago. What a glorious faith, what a glorious Church! What a privilege to belong to that Church!

Aim to instill these thoughts so deeply into the minds of the pupils that they will influence them for later life. Teach them gradually to follow the Mass intelligently and try to form in them the habit of praying the Mass with the priest.

Occasionally take the pupils by surprise by asking them questions about the Mass of the day; for example, the color of the vestment, the reason for the color, whether the Creed was said, how they could tell, etc.

*What Do You Say?*

In the Council of Nicaea the Church exercised her right to say what we must believe and what we must not believe. The problems are intended to bring out this right of the Church.

1. Jesus said: "He that heareth you heareth Me and he that despiseth you despiseth Me" (Luke x. 16). Discuss the significance of the text.

2. The Church has the power to make laws from Jesus Christ Himself. "Whatever you shall bind on earth shall be bound also in heaven." We read this quotation in the Bible mentioned by Ellen's grandmother. Stress here especially that as God's creatures, we owe Him worship, and that the Mass is the highest form of worship, because it is Jesus Himself who is offered to God. We should, therefore, go to Mass as an act of love, worship, adoration, etc., rather than just out of obedience to the Church's law.

3. Point out that the Church does not and cannot regulate all our daily actions. She teaches us what is right and what is wrong and then expects us to use our own judgment. The priest in St. Louis happens to know that the play, for some reason, is not good for people to see. He is giving them good advice. He is not pronouncing a teaching of the Church but he is acting as a good shepherd who loves and cares for his sheep. The priest in Chicago may not have had his attention called to this particular play, his congregation may not as a whole be of the movie-going kind, etc.

*Can You Answer These Questions?*

1. The Apostles' Creed.

2. The truths which the Church believes and teaches.

3. Jesus Christ Himself, when He said: "Going therefore, teach ye all nations."

4. Yes, the Church teaches the same thing at all times.

5. Yes.

6. Heresies.

7. No, the Church cannot err in matters of faith and morals.

8. The pope, or if he cannot be present, one of his representatives.

*Return to Introduction to This Unit:*

As a final summary or clinching or organization of this unit, return to its introductory statement and read it again and discuss in the light of all the material of the unit.

*Teacher's References:*

*Church History,* "The Council of Nicaea," pages 109–111.

*The Life of the Church,* Chap. III, Introduction, pages 126–128.

*Test Yourself:*

Vary the work on the different tests from time to time. Sometimes let the pupils ask one another and again hear the answers yourself.

1. St. Monica.
2. St. John.
3. St. Barnabas.
4. St. Augustine.
5. St. Ambrose.
6. St. Timothy.
7. St. Peter.
8. St. Stephen.
9. St. Justin and St. Clement of Alexandria.

*Teacher's Notes:*

# UNIT III

## HIDDEN HEROES OF CHRIST'S CHURCH

*Time:* First week in November.

### Feasts to Remember

November 1   Feast of All Saints

(Since the work of this year is developed largely through the biographies of the saints, a great deal of attention should be paid to this feast. You might celebrate it by some special little program in honor of each pupil's patron saint. See *Journal of Religious Instruction,* "Consider the Lives of the Saints," November, 1934.)

      2   Feast of All Souls

(Members of the Church Suffering. What can we do for them?)

      3   St. Charles Borromeo.

### *The Unit Introduction:*

Try to give the children a clear idea of the beginnings of monastic life and point out that our present convents are an outgrowth of this new form of life.

When you have completed the two lessons, come back to the introduction again and by means of questions assure yourself that the pupils have grasped the unit as a whole.

### Lesson 11

*Aim:* To learn from the life of St. Anthony how the hidden heroes of God's Church contributed their share to the growth and holiness of the Church by the prayers and penances which they performed for themselves and for other members of the Church Militant and Church Suffering.

*Preparation:* If possible have on hand a picture of a hermitage.

The story "Anselm and the Lizard" in *American Reader,* V, page 337, is very beautiful and will help to show how God rewards those who are devoted to Him. It should be read to the class by the teacher after the general discussion of hermit life.

### Read Lesson 11

Discuss the various steps toward the new kind of life. Anthony sold everything and left home. At first he lived alone. Later others settled around him. They lived in separate huts but were governed by him. They worked while they prayed for the common good. In the past men had lived by themselves alone. They were called *hermits.* Now for the first time they settled in groups, although still living alone. These men were called monks.

How did St. Anthony contribute his share to the life of the Church? By his holiness, his life of sacrifice and penance, his close union with Christ, the Vine, he was gaining merits which other members of the Mystical Body could share.

### Practical Application

Every day at Mass, the priest reads a selection from the New Testament. This story is called the Gospel. The Gospel is read at the left-hand side of the altar (the people's left), known as the Gospel side. Because the Gospel is the word of God (taken from the Bible) we stand respectfully while it is being read and listen with reverent attitude. At its beginning the priest signs himself with the sign of the cross and we should do the same, making the cross on the forehead, the lips, and the breast.

Teach the children always to listen to the Gospel with great respect.

Have them take notice from now on when the Gospel is read and sign themselves with the sign of the cross.

The Scripture texts used throughout the book are, it should be pointed out, taken from the Bible. Therefore they should always be recited with great reverence.

The little situations are to be talked over with the children.

They are intended to bring out the true spirit of the Church in regard to penance.

1. John ought to eat what is placed before him. He is really not doing penance but his own will. What might he do that hurts, without injuring his health?

2. If Ellen does this for the love of God, she is gaining in two ways. How?

3. The mother's suggestion is wise. Francis' idea is very foolish. Discuss. It is the effort we make that counts.

4. She is doing the act out of fear of pain and not out of love of God.

5. This is a very good act of penance.

6. Both penitential and practical. It is practices such as these that should be encouraged. They are an excellent aid in the formation of character.

7. Help by a practical suggestion: "Dear God, I do not want to have these thoughts of jealousy. I want to be glad with others when they are praised. Help me."

8. A good penance and an aid to good health.

9. If both do it with an equally good intention, May makes by far the greater sacrifice.

10. Helen is looking for praise. She is not doing penance.

11. Mollie needs the milk for her body. She is not wise in her choice.

12. Make ejaculations and gain indulgences in other ways. (Review some of the simpler ejaculations, such as, "My Jesus, mercy!"; "Jesus, Mary, and Joseph.")

Teach little acts of love, sorrow, etc., which the children can use at any time.

Plan to correlate this lesson with geography. The making of paper and linen could well be taken up at this time in a simple way, possibly through a little extra reading on the subject.

*Things to Do:*

1. An activity such as this serves as a good example of what to do and what to leave undone. The making of a hermitage has

its mechanical advantages, of course, but unless the connection is made with the lesson, it serves no purpose here. If a child brings a good model it may be exhibited in the classroom. The children should all know why it is called a hermitage, why hermits lived alone, and how they spent their time, etc.

3, 4, and 5. Correlation with geography, composition, and reading.

4. January 17, white vestment, because he is not a martyr.

*Can You Answer These Questions?*

1. God punishes us for sin because in committing it we offend Him and break His laws. We are also punished when we break the laws of the state or the country.

2. We can satisfy or make up to God for temporal punishment due to sin by acts of penance and mortification, by prayer, good works, and indulgences, by hearing Mass, and receiving the sacraments.

3. Only the eternal punishment for sin is forgiven when we receive absolution.

4. Temporal punishment is forgiven by indulgences, good works, sacraments, etc.

5. Penance of the right kind is not harmful but helpful to us.

6. We must avoid anything that would be harmful either to the body or the soul.

Point out in a general way, that even priests of God can go wrong. God gave all men free will, so that they can choose to do either good or evil. Otherwise they could not earn heaven. Popes, bishops, and priests receive many special graces from God. Therefore, if they become bad, their punishment will be the greater. The higher a person stands, the greater will be his fall.

The pope, however, can never lead the Church away from God, no matter what his own personal faults may be. God promised to be with His Church until the end of time.

Be sure that the children understand that the "storms" which the Church had to go through were difficulties.

*Teacher's References:*

*Church History,* "Asceticism," page 89.

*Catholic Action Series,* Book II, "Training the Passions," pages 341 and 342.

*The Life of the Church,* "Monasticism," pages 140–146.

*Teacher's Notes:*

## Lesson 12

*Aim:* To learn how St. Benedict developed the monastic life, which has added so many holy and learned men and women to the Church; and also to understand from him how important it is to flee from sin and bad companions.

*Preparation:* Have pictures handy of Benedictine monks and nuns, also of some of the old monasteries. Have one or more pupils prepared to relate the life of St. Scholastica to the class.

Words to explain:

*Abbot:* The superior or head of a group of monks is sometimes called abbot. A house which is ruled over by an abbot or abbess (a woman) is known as an *abbey*. The Benedictines use these terms.

*To become perfect:* to do everything in the way most pleasing to God.

As we have already seen, the Church is made up of all kinds of people just as the vine is made up of different parts, such as branches and leaves and fruits and tendrils of various sizes. Sometimes the Church has needed whole armies of real soldiers to help her fight her enemies. With St. Anthony there grew up another great army in the Church, an army of men and women who spent their time in prayer and penance, in study and work. Today we shall learn of the work of St. Benedict, one of the early monks, through whom the great army of monks and nuns grew so strong that it began to spread over the whole Church.

*Read Lesson 12*

Talk about the lesson. Point out that Benedict's prayer was humble. He did not believe he could work a miracle by his own strength. He asked God to do it for him.

*Practical Application*

Dwell on the evil of sin and show what constitutes an approximate occasion of sin.

The problem is intended to bring out the point that one good apple in a barrel of bad ones cannot make the bad ones good.

*Things to Do:*

1. If there are Benedictines in the vicinity make it a point to have the children see them.

3. St. Benedict, March 21; St. Scholastica, February 10. White vestments are worn.

4. Use this occasion to review the qualities of a good prayer. We must pray with devotion, humility, confidence, resignation, and perseverance.

5. See Teacher's References.

*Can You Answer These Questions?*

1. Sin is a willful breaking of the Law of God; that is, of the Ten Commandments, and the Commandments of the Church.

2. We should avoid sin because it offends God who is our Father, because it is the greatest evil in the world, and because through it we may lose our souls.

3. We should avoid sin by prayer, by receiving the sacraments often, by keeping away from the occasion of sin, and by trying to love God more and more.

Point out to the pupils often that if we love God very much we shall keep away from sin because we do not wish to hurt Him.

4. The proximate occasion of sin may be a person, a place, or a thing which causes us to fall into sin.

5. A sin is mortal when the wrong we commit is a serious matter; when we have had time to think about it; and when we have consented to do it.

6. A sin is venial when the wrong we commit is not serious.

7. Mortal sin

   *a*) Robs us of sanctifying grace,

   *b*) Deprives us of all heavenly merits, and

   *c*) Places us in danger of everlasting death.

8. When we have committed a mortal sin we should make a good act of contrition and go to confession as soon as we have a chance.

9. *a*) Examine our conscience.

   *b*) Make an act of contrition.

   *c*) Have a firm purpose of amendment.

*d*) Confess our sins to the priest.

*e*) Make satisfaction, or perform the penance given to us.
Other questions such as the following may be added if desired:
What does the sacrament of penance do for us?

Who gave the priest the power to forgive sins? (John xx. 22, 23.)

What examples of sorrow for sin can you give from the Bible
(Peter, Magdalen, the Prodigal Son, the Good Thief)?

*Return to Introduction to This Unit:*

As a final summary or clinching or organization of this unit,
return to its introductory statement and read it again and
discuss in the light of all the material of the unit.

*Teacher's References:*

*Church History,* "St. Benedict of Nursia," pages 183–188;
"The Pontificate of St. Gregory the Great," pages 192–199.

*Catholic Action Series,* Book I, Chap. XI, "Sin and Temptation."

*The Life of the Church,* "The Monks of the West — St.
Benedict," page 165.

*Test Yourself:*

(Answers)

1. Communion of Saints.
2. Pentecost.
3. 3,000.
4. Jerusalem.
5. Paul.
6. Timothy.
7. 72.
8. Catacombs.
9. Augustine.
10. Constantine.
11. Nicene.
12. Anthony.
13. Benedict.
14. Peter and Paul.

*Teacher's Notes:*

# UNIT IV

# THE CHURCH IN THE MIDDLE AGES

*Time:* From the second week in November to the second week in December.

## Feasts to Remember

November *15 St. Albert the Great
        (Teacher of St. Thomas Aquinas.)
    *21 Presentation of the Blessed Virgin Mary
        (Sing a hymn in honor of Mary.)
    *22 St. Caecilia
        (Patròness of Music. One of the early martyrs.)
    *30 St. Andrew, Apostle
        (Let the pupils tell where he labored for the
        spread of the Church and how he died.)
December * 3 St. Francis Xavier
        (Patron of the Missions, Apostle of India. Text,
        Lesson 32.)

## *The Unit Introduction:*

If possible, the teacher should read one of the references and tell the story of the Migration of Nations more at length.

For the second time, now, the branches of the great Vine seemed to have been hopelessly destroyed. When did it seem that way the first time? Recall the coin which Diocletian had made, and the words he had engraved upon it. After the Migration of Nations everything seemed again to be destroyed. But the branches of the great Vine grew up more full of life and strength than ever. The missionaries, the successors of the Apostles, converted the barbarians. The work took hundreds of years. Finally, however, all of Europe became Christian. The great Vine was beautiful to behold. It spread out its branches in all

72

directions. It bore the precious fruit that made the Middle Ages in many ways the most glorious of all times.

When the four lessons have been studied, return to read this page again, and have the children show by specific examples how the Church inspired her children to do great deeds and to live and die for the glory of God (Charlemagne, Crusaders, St. Louis).

## Lesson 13

*Aim:* To show how the Church and the State worked hand in hand during the reign of the great emperor Charlemagne.

*Preparation:* Broaden your own knowledge on the subject in hand by reading some of the references.

Look over the "Things to Do" and be prepared for all the activities the children are to undertake.

As an approach to this lesson have the class dramatize the first paragraph of the story, ending with a hymn of praise, such as "Holy God." With the enthusiasm of the Roman people fresh in mind, proceed with the story.

*Read Lesson 13*

What were some of the powers the pope had which the emperor had not? The pope could consecrate bishops, explain the teachings of the Church, forgive sins, etc.

What were some of the powers the emperor had? He could make laws to protect the people's life and property. He could call out the men to fight for their country and also for the pope if necessary, etc.

Note especially that Charlemagne attended Mass whenever possible.

Call special attention to Charlemagne's interest in education. When we consider that even now, after more than a thousand years, there are many children who do not have a chance to study, we can see better what a far-seeing and wise emperor Charlemagne was.

In connection with the last paragraph speak of Holy Viaticum, ordinarily the last Holy Communion a person receives on earth, and show that it is a special grace to receive our Lord just before death.

Make much of good citizenship from the point of view of Christianity.

*Ask Yourself:*

Try to make the children understand the intimate connection between good citizenship and true Christianity. All authority comes from God. Without God there can be no law or order. Endeavor also to instill into them a deep respect for authority and law. Getting away without being caught, crossing the street when the traffic signal says "Stop," may seem insignificant to the child, but the underlying principle, obedience to lawful authority, is a serious matter. Show how little acts of disobedience pave the way for greater. Prove by examples that criminals are usually people who broke the law in small things when they were young.

Sometimes children are encouraged or even taught by parents or elders to disobey the law. Be very tactful in bringing this point home to the children. Sometimes older people do not understand it that way. They did not all have the chance to go to a good Catholic school or they have forgotten what they were taught. But that does not excuse us. We know now what God expects of us and we must try our best to do what is right.

Point out also the evil that would result if *all* people broke laws without concern.

This lesson offers many opportunities for the development of good citizenship.

Have on the bulletin board a picture of the President and also of other outstanding citizens known to the children. Under the pictures might be added such words as the following: "The best citizen is he that serves God best."

*What Do You Say?*

The problem should be thoroughly discussed. It should bring out the thought that "as the twig is bent the tree inclines." Both good and bad habits are formed by degrees.

*Things to Do:*

1. Let the whole class join in a song of praise, the "Holy God," *"Laudate,"* or a similar hymn.

2. Also called Aachen.

3. Let the children read this lesson as a private assignment if desired.

4. Connect this activity with the lesson. The rule shows how interested Charlemagne was in all phases of public and private life.

5. Our Lord's own words when He died on the cross.

6. Take a few outstanding characteristics in particular; especially honesty, trust in divine Providence, love of fellow men.

7. The pupils might find their opposites also, to bring out the contrast more strongly.

8. Let the children choose what they like best.

9. Recall these texts again as the occasion presents itself.

10. Repeat this exercise during the week.

11. An excellent activity that may be carried out more at length.

*Can You Answer These Questions?*

1. The Fourth Commandment requires obedience to all who have authority over us.

2. Yes, just the same as other people.

3. Yes, they, too, must obey the laws of God.

4. God, whose place they take.

5. Jesus Christ, when He said: "Whatsoever you shall bind on earth shall be bound also in heaven; and whatsoever you shall loose upon earth shall be loosed also in heaven."

6. The Corporal Works of Mercy.

7. To feed the hungry.

8. To give drink to the thirsty.

*Teacher's References:*

*Church History,* Chapter VI, "The Age of Charlemagne."

*Catholic Action Series,* Book II, "Members of Church and State," pages 308–317.

*Teacher's Notes:*

## Lesson 14

*Aim:* To show why the Christians venerated the Holy Land and why they desired to free it from the hands of the Turks.

*Preparation:* If there are places of historical interest in your vicinity, get pictures and other information about them. Talk about them to the class and try to make them understand why these places are held in veneration. Then show how the Church has more reason than anyone else to live and venerate the places where our Lord and His Holy Mother lived and died.

*Read Lesson 14*

Study the map and have the children locate some of the holy places they would like to visit and tell why. This can be made an interesting and profitable activity in connection with the story. Refer to the way of the cross, which is a kind of pilgrimage to the places where our Lord suffered.

If you have not mentioned the fact before, call attention to the altar stone which must contain relics of martyrs.

*Things to Do:*

1. Spend just enough time on this to show how people venerate places associated with important people or events. Use the history period, if necessary.

2, 3, 4. Associate these activities closely with the lesson itself.

5. If possible, show the children a relic in its case.

6. If you make the stations as a group, be sure to use very simple prayers, so as to make this activity impressive. Remember you are aiming to form good habits. Let the pupils keep in mind that they are walking the road to Calvary. The inexpensive little book *The Stations of the Cross* for children (Paulist Press) is excellent.

*Can You Answer These Questions?*

1. In order to redeem us; that is, to open heaven which was closed by the sin of our first parents.

2. Because the saints are the friends of God who sanctified their bodies on earth by using them for God's honor and glory.

3. No, not all people go straight to heaven when they die.

4. Those who die with mortal sin on their souls go to hell, those with venial sins go to purgatory.

5. We may not expose ourselves to danger unnecessarily.

6. That would be a sin of presumption.

7. We are commanded to keep from injury our own or our neighbor's body or soul.

Questions referring to the veneration of saints and relics may be added here if desired.

*Teacher's References:*

*Church History*, "Mohammedanism and the Church," Chapter IV.

*Catholic Action Series*, Book II, "The Symbolism of the Parish Altar," etc.

*Teacher's Notes:*

## Lesson 15

*Aim:* To learn about the Crusades, the holy wars which the Crusaders undertook for the delivery of the Holy Land.

*Preparation:* Bring to your aid as many pictures of knights and crusaders as you possibly can, especially "Sir Galahad" by Watts.

Introduce the lesson by letting the children tell something they have read about brave knights, and show how knighthood reached its highest ideals by fighting for the cause of Christ.

*Read Lesson 15*

Show how far the crusaders had to travel, and give some estimate of the time it might have taken to go on horseback and by ship from France to Jerusalem. (See references.)

The crusades were not undertaken in quick succession. In all, they lasted several hundred years.

The Orders of Christian Knights were like orders of monks. The knights made a special vow to fight for the Holy Land or for the rights of the Church.

Explain more at length the good results of the crusades:

They united the Christian nations more closely. Often these nations were at war with one another. When they were called to the crusades they forgot their own quarrels and went side by side to fight for the cause of the Church.

The Turks knew a great deal about medicine, architecture, etc., some of which the people of the Christian countries knew little about. The crusaders brought home many new ideas from the East.

The crusades were followed shortly by the invention of printing, the discovery of America, etc., all an indirect result of the newly awakened desire for adventure and learning.

*Practical Application*

Boys and girls will delight in pretending that they are real knights and ladies. Teach them that true knighthood consists in doing what is noble and honorable. Let them choose Christ as their leader and have them pick out certain qualities that they will strive to practice.

80     FIFTH GRADE MANUAL

Discuss the suggestions. Encourage the pupils to make frequent visits to the Blessed Sacrament all by themselves. Perhaps you can teach them here how to converse quietly with God. Occasionally suggest to groups or individuals to talk some particular problem over with God. In this way you will help them form habits of prayer and intimate conversation with God.

Make a special study of knighthood during this and the following week, using largely your English, reading, history, and geography periods.

*Things to Do:*

2. An opportunity to correlate a bit of geography.

4. Just by way of getting a clearer mental picture.

5. This would make an excellent booklet cover for a study of knighthood.

6. It would be well just to read selections to the class.

7. See the list of "Good Things to Read."

*Can You Answer These Questions?*

1. It means that we should keep His commandments and do all that His Church tells us to do.

2. God watches over us and cares for us at all times.

3. Evil came into the world as a result of the sin of our first parents. God allows us to be tried by evil to prove our love and loyalty to Him but nothing can harm our souls against our own will. God draws good out of evil as the story of Joseph of Egypt shows.

4. A guardian angel.

5. The angels watch over us and warn us against sin and evil.

6. God made the angels.

7. They did not all remain good. Some of them sinned and were thrown into hell.

8. They are called evil spirits or devils.

9. They try to harm us by tempting us to commit sin.

Review in general "The Angels" and God's Providence.

*Teacher's References:*

*Church History,* "The Crusades and the Military Orders," page 311.

*Catholic Action Series,* Book III, Chapter 1.

*Teacher's Notes:*

## Lesson 16

*Aim:* To learn from the life of King Louis how the Christian knights often aided the cause of the Church, not only by their swords but also by the sanctity of their own lives.

*Preparation:* Let the children collect pictures, tell stories, and read books about noble knights. Be sure, however, not to lose sight of the religious ideal. The knights, as we learn from the crusades, stood for faith, respect for virtue, and charity to the poor and needy. Secular stories of knighthood often overlook the higher ideals for which knighthood originally stood.

*Read Lesson 16*

Explain any words or sentences that may not be entirely clear.

Talk especially about the character traits that stand out so brilliantly in the life of St. Louis.

Point out from the incidents in the lesson that it takes courage to do the right and show how even in little things a great deal of courage may be required to act on principle.

*Ask Yourself:*

Often children have the idea that certain actions are permissible as long as they are not caught in the act, or that wrong may be done because the end to be attained is good. Although not all the problems deal directly with sin, the teacher will have an opportunity here to impress deeply upon the children the fact that a sin is never allowed, no matter how good the intention. Sin is the greatest evil in the world because it is an offense against God. We may never offend God.

Point out that in order to become strong characters the children should begin here and now to train themselves in little things for the great things that will be expected of them in the future.

*Things to Do:*

1. Preferably the scene with his mother, in order to impress it deeply upon the minds of the children.

2. Why did the crusaders stop in Africa first?

3. Perhaps a story can be planned first and then the play written from it.

4. Choose one of the best letters to read to the class.

5. The children might devise a banner for themselves as a pledge of their loyalty to Christ their leader.

*Can You Answer These Questions?*

1. Three things are necessary to make a sin mortal.

   *a)* A serious matter,

*b*) Sufficient reflection,

*c*) Full consent of the will.

2. No, we may not commit a sin to save our life.

3. Sin is the greatest evil in the world. We cannot, therefore, say it is not so bad to commit a venial sin.

(Deal here with the chief results of mortal sin and the chief results of venial sin. Mortal sin robs us of sanctifying grace; deprives us of all heavenly merits; places us in danger of everlasting death.)

4. Venial sin lessens the love of God in our heart; makes us less worthy of His graces; weakens our will power; little by little leads to mortal sin.

5. He should go to confession at once, or, if he has not the chance, make an act of perfect contrition with a desire to confess as soon as possible.

(See whether the children remember the difference between perfect and imperfect contrition.)

*Return to Introduction to This Unit:*

As a final summary or clinching or organization of this unit, return to its introductory statement and read it again and discuss in the light of all the material of the unit.

*Teacher's References:*

*Catholic Action Series*, Book I, "Sin and Temptation," pages 144–149; Book III, "Training for Catholic Action," pages 23–45.

*Test Yourself:*

(Answers)

| | |
|---|---|
| 1. The Blessed Virgin Mary. | 10. St. Veronica. |
| 2. St. Peter. | 11. St. Thomas. |
| 3. St. Paul. | 12. St. Helena. |
| 4. St. Andrew. | 13. St. Joseph. |
| 5. St. Blanche. | 14. St. Monica. |
| 6. St. Caecilia. | 15. St. Stephen. |
| 7. St. John. | 16. St. Joachim. |
| 8. St. John the Baptist. | 17. St. Anthony. |
| 9. St. Anne. | 18. St. Benedict. |

19. St. Agnes.
20. St. Mary Magdalen.
21. St. Blase.
22. St. Augustine.

23. St. Louis.
24. St. Timothy.
25. St. Matthias.

*Teacher's Notes:*

# UNIT V

## GREAT POPES OF THE MIDDLE AGES

*Time:* Second Week in December.

### Feasts to Remember

| | | |
|---|---|---|
| December | *7 | St. Ambrose, Doctor of the Church (Baptized St. Augustine. See Lesson 8.) |
| | *8 | Immaculate Conception (Prepare a program in honor of Mary Immaculate. See Lesson 35.) |
| | *13 | St. Lucy (Lesson 39.) |

The little Advent practices usually performed by the children at this season should, if possible, have a bearing on the religion lesson of the week. For example, the suggestions on page 106 may well be carried out in honor of the Infant Saviour.

### The Unit Introduction:

Explanations will be necessary to clear the way for the next lessons. Charlemagne and the popes worked together, we recall, for the good of all concerned. Not all kings were as great and good as Charlemagne. Sometimes the rulers wanted to govern not only the State but the Church as well. Great trials for the Church were the result.

Recall the Storm at Sea when the Apostles thought all was lost. That is the way people must have felt at times when unworthy leaders ruled and seemed to triumph in the world. Two popes stand out especially during these times. They were great champions for the rights of the Church. Although things looked very dark, Christ's promise, "I shall be with you," was again verified.

Use the introduction again to summarize the unit at the end of the week. Keep in mind that every story has a close bearing on the unit as a whole and every unit again on the main topic of the year, The Vine and the Branches.

### Lesson 17

*Aim:* To learn from Pope Gregory VII the evils that threatened the Church in his time and how by strength of character and the guidance of the Holy Ghost, he fought against them.

*Preparation:* Explain in a simple way, that the election of a new pope or the appointment of bishops, pastors, etc., is the business of the Church. When a bishop or a priest is needed today, for a certain position, he is appointed by the Church. No president or king or governor has anything to say about it. In the time of Gregory VII kings and princes wanted the right to say who should be the bishops in their country. We can easily see that a king would not know best who should hold so holy an office. Only the pope and his counselors have a right to say. This question was one of the difficulties of the reign of Gregory. It took a strong man to fight against the powerful kings and princes.

Explain the following words:

*Excommunicate:* to take away the privilege of being a child of the Church. The Church sometimes does to some of her disobedient children what parents do at times when they send away a child from the family and refuse to call it their own child until it obeys the will of the parents.

*Exile:* to send a person out of his own country.

### Read Lesson 17

"Gregory began at once to make war on all who were guilty," means that he fought for the rights of the Church not by actual warfare but by punishing the guilty and forcing them to come to time.

Note that even kings must obey the laws of God and of the Church.

How could Gregory win the victory, since he died before the

struggle ended? He saw the great difficulty and fought it with all his might. When he died, the Church had become strong enough to continue the fight to the end.

*Ask Yourself:*

Show by these points that one becomes strong to fight evil by being prepared for it, by daily *action.*

Discuss King Henry's disposition when he asked forgiveness of his wrongs. Make clear here that God sees the heart and that a sin is *not* forgiven unless the penitent is sincere in his desire to amend. A penitent can deceive the priest, but in that case the absolution, which the priest gives in the name of God, will have no effect.

*Can You Answer These Questions?*

1. The pope, the bishop of Rome, is the visible head of the Church.

2. Jesus Christ made him the visible ruler when He appointed Peter and his successors as head of the Church.

3. The sacrament of penance.

4. Our contrition must come from the heart and not merely from the lips.

It should be prompted by right motives, that is, we should be sorry on account of God's goodness or justice.

It should cover all our mortal sins without exception.

It must be greater for sin than for any other thing.

5. Henry was not sincere. He had no firm purpose not to commit sin again.

6. We must confess all our mortal sins.

7. We must perform the penance the priest gives us and be determined never to sin again.

8. A person excommunicated is no longer acknowledged as a child of the Church. He cannot receive the sacraments until he does what the Church asks him.

9. Simony is selling holy things, such as, an office, a blessing, or a blessed article, for money.

10. As a usual thing it is practiced by buying and selling blessed articles.

*Teacher's References:*

*The Life of the Church,* "The Church and the Kingdom of God," pages 168–174.

*Church History,* "Hildebrand as Pope Gregory," Chap. VII, pages 304–310.

*Catholic Action Series,* Book III, "Training for Catholic Action," pages 23–59.

*Teacher's Notes:*

**Lesson 18**

*Aim:* To learn how, nearly a hundred years after Pope Gregory VII, Pope Innocent III had again to struggle against powerful kings and princes, and how carefully he guarded the Church and strengthened her position.

*Preparation:* If possible have pictures of the Vatican garden and of the Church of the Lateran to show.

Explain: *Lateran Church:* the oldest church in Rome, therefore also called the mother of all churches. At that time it was also the pope's cathedral.

*Protested:* spoke against.

*Sancto Spiritu:* Holy Spirit. We must remember that there were no regularly organized hospitals such as we have today.

By way of approach to the new story you might review the lesson of the Council of Nicaea. There were, of course, other councils since then, about which we have not heard. The next council we shall read about was the Fourteenth General Council, and the fourth held at the Lateran.

*Read Lesson 18*

Discuss the scenes between the pope and St. Francis. St. Francis had come to ask the pope to approve his Order. We must remember that then, as now, people thought a great deal of fine clothing. Anyone who appeared as St. Francis did would not, at first sight, make a favorable impression.

It was the Order of St. Francis with that of St. Dominic that helped to keep the Church from falling; that is, from losing many of its children through heresy, and its rights through selfish princes and kings.

The opening of the story offers opportunity for dramatization.

Locate the Strait of Gibraltar.

Discuss how it came that there was no law of the Church before the year 1215 requiring that Holy Communion be received once a year. It was not necessary before; just as fifty years ago traffic signals were unnecessary.

Speak here of the necessity of frequent Holy Communion. In

fact, our part in the Sacrifice of the Mass is not really complete unless we partake also of the banquet, which is Holy Communion. If we are to acquire strength for our journey on the highway to heaven, we must have food for our souls.

### Do You Do Your Duty?

Discuss the specific duties of the children.

Their principal duty is to obey those who have authority over them. This gives an opportunity for a thorough review of the Fourth Commandment. Whenever there is question of some resolution to be made by the children, be as specific as you can.

Avoid general resolutions such as "I will be good today." Give the children time to talk and think over their duties. Then tell them to examine themselves to see whether there is some important duty, such as not doing some little piece of work assigned them at home, that they have not been performing well. Have each child think of one duty he is going to do well today. Remind them of it before they go home and ask on the following day whether they remembered. Do not make them tell publicly whether they have forgotten or not, but encourage them to try again.

In all cases where such little resolutions are made, the following suggestions should be kept in mind:

1. Be sure the children know exactly what is expected of them.

2. Lead them to choose a specific practice that applies particularly to themselves.

3. Follow up the thought during the day, especially before dismissal and ask about it in the morning in some such way as the following: "I wonder how many of you thought of your little practice yesterday. I hope you all did. I think I see one little boy who forgot. But he is going to try ever so much harder today so he can tell Jesus tonight that he kept his resolution."

4. Whenever possible go through the action instead of just saying what is to be done. For example, the children have decided to practice acts of politeness today. Try some of them out immediately by dramatization, choosing acts such as the class needs

most to practice; for example, opening the door for another, saying "please" and "thank you," etc.

The duty of being a good parishioner may well be stressed at this time also, especially the following points:

Reverence to the priests and sisters, contributing to Sunday collection, etc.

Boys tipping hat when passing church and girls bowing their heads, showing interest in all that concerns the Church.

4. If there is time, the story of Ruth may be told. Ruth became the wife of Booz because he noticed her fidelity to her duty. Through that marriage she became the greatgrandmother of the great king David from whose family Jesus was born.

The children will find many stories in other readers that bring out fidelity to duty. Give them the pleasure of finding such stories themselves and, if there is time, of dramatizing the simpler ones.

*Can You Answer These Questions?*

1. The first three Commandments of God.
2. The Fourth Commandment of the Church.
3. The Fifth Commandment of the Church.
4. We should receive Holy Communion as often as we can, if possible every day.
5. *a*) State of grace,
   *b*) Fasting from midnight,
   *c*) The proper reverence and disposition.
6. *Before Communion:*
   (1) Be sure you have no mortal sin on your soul.
   (2) Go to confession if you have a mortal sin on your soul.
   (3) Do not eat or drink anything from midnight on.
   (4) Prepare your soul for the coming of Jesus:
      *a*) Think of Jesus and talk to Him.
      *b*) Tell Him you love Him.
      *c*) Tell Him you are sorry for your sins.
      *d*) Tell Him you want Him to come to you.
   *At Holy Communion:*
   (1) Go to the rail with hands folded and eyes cast down.

(2) All the time keep thinking of Jesus.

(3) When your turn comes, put back your head and put out your tongue.

(4) Swallow the Sacred Host as soon as you can.

(5) Walk back to your place slowly and do not look around.

*After Holy Communion:*

(1) Remember Jesus is in your heart.

(2) Tell Him again how much you love Him.

(3) Tell Him you are glad He came into your heart.

(4) Tell Him about yourself, your lessons, your sins, your little secrets.

(5) Ask Him to bless your parents, your teachers, and your friends.

*And Remember:*

(1) Do not leave the church for at least ten minutes after Holy Communion.

(2) Use your prayer book if you cannot think of more to say.

(3) Never touch the Sacred Host with the fingers. If it sticks to your mouth, loosen it with your tongue and swallow it.

(4) Invite Jesus to come to you soon again.

7. Jesus Christ gave the Church the right to make laws. (Ask for Scripture Text.)

8. Jesus Christ in His sermon on the mount.

9. In the Eight Beatitudes.

10. Show how children can be peacemakers.

### Return to Introduction to This Unit:

As a final summary or clinching or organization of this unit, return to its introductory statement and read it again and discuss in the light of all the material of the unit.

### Teacher's References:

*Church History,* "The Papacy at the Noontide of Its Power," pages 341–346.

*Catholic Action Series,* Book I, "Nourishing the Life of the Soul," Chap. XIV.

*Teacher's Notes:*

*Can You Find Them?*

Since it will be impossible for all children to look for these texts, unless they have a Bible at home, give each child a text to find at least several times in the course of the year, so that all may learn what it is about.

The following sentences are all taken from Holy Scripture. Look for them in the Holy Bible and tell something about the story. Numbers 2 and 4 are taken from epistles. Tell to whom and by whom they were written.

1. If thou wilt be perfect, go sell what thou hast, and give to the poor, and thou shalt have treasure in heaven, and come, follow Me (Matt. xix. 21). (Christ to the rich young man.)

2. Without faith it is impossible to please God (Heb. xi. 6). (St. Paul's letter to the Hebrews.)

3. He that heareth you, heareth Me; and he that despiseth you, despiseth Me; and he that despiseth Me, despiseth Him that sent Me (Luke x. 16). (Christ to the Apostles.)

4. There are three who give testimony in heaven, the Father, the Word, and the Holy Ghost. And these three are one (I John v. 7). (Epistle of St. John to the early Christians.)

5. Thomas answered and said to Him: My Lord and my God. (John xx. 28). (St. Thomas, the Apostle, to Jesus after His resurrection.)

6. All power is given to Me in heaven and in earth (Matt. xxviii. 18). (Christ to His Apostles.)

7. And suddenly there came a sound from heaven, as of a mighty wind coming, and it filled the whole house where they were sitting (Acts ii. 2). (St. Luke in the Acts of the Apostles — the book of early Church history.)

8. And there appeared to them parted tongues as it were of fire, and it sat upon every one of them, and they were all filled with the Holy Ghost (Acts ii. 3). (St. Luke in the Acts of the Apostles.)

9. If thou wilt enter into life, keep the commandments (Matt. xix. 17). (Christ to the rich young man.)

10. For what doth it profit a man, if he gain the whole world, and suffer the loss of his own soul (Matt. xvi. 26)? (Christ to His disciples.)

# UNIT VI

## GREAT SAINTS OF THE MIDDLE AGES

*Time:* Third week in December and first and second weeks in January.

### Feasts to Remember

December *21  St. Thomas, Apostle.
(Have the pupils tell where he worked for the spread of the faith. It was he who used the words "My Lord and my God!" On what occasion?)

     25  Christmas

   *26  St. Stephen
(Lesson 4)

   *27  St. John, Apostle
(Where did he preach the faith? Was he a martyr?)

    28  Holy Innocents

January    1  The Circumcision

     2  Holy Name of Jesus

     6  Epiphany
(The three wise men must have carried the faith back with them to the East and so prepared the way for the Apostles.)

     7  Holy Family

*The Unit Introduction:*

Recall at the opening of the new unit that the early monks spent their time in prayer and work, away from the noise and trouble of the world. Later some of them went out into pagan lands to convert the nations to Christianity. During the Middle Ages it became necessary to go out among the Christians themselves to preach against the evils of the day.

Recall to the minds of the pupils the dream of Pope Innocent III. The Church seemed on the point of falling into a heap of ruins. A great army of men was needed to come to the assistance of the pope, so that, by their preaching and other good works they might uphold and strengthen the tottering walls.

It is of these outstanding men and their followers that the unit treats. Enumerate them again at the end of the unit and show how they contributed their share to bring help and strength to the Church.

## Lesson 19

*Aim:* To learn through the lesson of St. Bernard, about the life and work of those who have followed a religious vocation and so joined the great spiritual army for the help and support of the Church.

*Preparation:* Find pictures pertaining to the lesson, especially of the Cathedral of Speyer and of Christ knocking at the door. Also saints or religious wearing habits of different orders.

Recall by means of questions, the beginnings and development of monastic life.

*Read Lesson 19*

Explain such expressions as the following:

"Now you will be heir to everything" — now you will get all the land and money that we would have shared, had we remained at home.

"Perfect monk" — one who keeps his rule and does everything as well as he can.

Have the children show, as they read the story, how much more

Bernard was able to do for God and the Church, by giving up everything that was near and dear to him.

Refer again to the first crusade and Pope Urban's fiery plea for help.

*Practical Application*

Make a very simple explanation of the meaning of religious life. Point out again the fact that the religious look for no reward in this world but in the next. You might talk more at length about the order or orders best known to the children.

Remind the children occasionally to pray in the words of St. Paul, "Lord, what wilt Thou have me do?" or in the words of little Samuel, "Speak, Lord, for Thy servant hears."

Since this is the Christmas season, dwell on the poverty in which Jesus came to earth and show how the monks and later also the nuns tried to imitate Him by taking the vow of poverty.

*Things to Do:*

1. Do not spend much extra time learning the names of the different orders now.

2. A little talk about the founder or foundress would be in order here.

3. Or, write a little vocation play based on the experience of St. Bernard when he made known his purpose to his parents and friends.

4. August 20.

5, 6. Be sure to explain the words of the *Memorare*. A prayer is never lost. It will be answered in some way although perhaps not in the way we expect. The Blessed Mother in particular has never forsaken anyone who has called on her. You might occasionally remind the pupils of the prayer and use it in school on feasts of the Blessed Virgin if it is not a part of the regular school prayers.

7. The words occur in the life of St. Anthony, Lesson 11.

8. Since we are going to have a special lesson on great cathedrals, it would be well to have a short report about this one as a preparation for what is to follow.

9. Not too much time need be spent on this list which may,

by the way, serve as a spelling list. It is intended to give a clearer understanding of the word *vocation*.

10. Recall what this title of "Doctor" means, by reviewing Lesson 8.

### Can You Answer These Questions?

1. Vocation means a "calling" for a particular state of life or work. A religious vocation means a calling to lead the life devoted especially to the work of God in a religious house such as a convent.

2. It was not right for anyone to try to keep Bernard from serving God as a religious.

3. A vow is a solemn promise to God to do or keep from doing something for love of Him.

4. Not anyone can take a vow. The confessor would have to be asked.

5. The Church has a right to release a person from his vows but ordinarily a vow made according to the laws of the Church may not be broken.

If possible, teach the hymn of St. Bernard. It is the *Jesu Dulcis Memoria*. Use it on the Feast of the Holy Name.

### Teacher's References:

*The Life of the Church,* "St. Bernard," pages 183–186.

*Church History,* "St. Bernard of Clairvaux," pages 321–326.

*Catholic Action Series,* Book III, "The Religious Life," pages 154–155.

### Teacher's Notes:

## Lesson 20

*Aim:* To learn from the life of St. Francis of Assisi how he raised up a great spiritual army of soldiers to assist the Church at a time when she seemed to be in danger.

*Preparation:* There are many beautiful stories and pictures relating to St. Francis of Assisi. Bring out especially during this season the story of his representation of the Nativity scene. *Six O'Clock Saints,* by Joan Windham (Sheed & Ward), tells the story very effectively for young children.

### Read Lesson 20

Refer to Lesson 18 to show the connection. Again we see how one man, filled with the love of God and his fellow men, became a strong helper in the cause of the Church.

Explain that love of poverty does not necessarily mean going in rags. A person may be well dressed and still love poverty. It means to try to get along with as little as possible for one's self for the love of God, in order the better to be able to help others with what one saves. Accordingly, a rich person may also practice poverty.

Explain also the following expressions: "Chose poverty as his companion and friend" — loved and practiced poverty all his life; "Put a price on every Christian head" — offered a reward for every Christian that was killed.

### Practical Application

The problems are intended to show how our actions influence others. Let the children talk about them freely and add other examples to the list. Such little problems become a great help in training character, provided the teacher has opportunity to assist the children individually and does so with a great deal of sympathy and tact.

### Things to Do:

1. Add other stories of hermits, if there is time.

2. Have pictures ready to show.

3. See reading list in text and Teacher's References.

7, 8. Kindness to animals may be made a special topic in connection with this lesson. Correlate the work with other subjects.

9. Take this opportunity to draw attention to beauties of nature.

10. St. Clare, August 12.

12. See Reading List.

### Can You Answer These Questions?

1. The soul is more important than the body. (St. Francis proved this truth by his life.)

2. The soul is a spirit which cannot die and which was created by God according to His own image and likeness.

3. Grace gives supernatural life to the soul.

4. There are two kinds of grace, sanctifying grace and actual grace.

5. Sanctifying grace is lost to the soul by mortal sin.

6. The Spiritual Works of Mercy.

7. To warn sinners,
   To instruct the ignorant,
   To counsel the doubting,
   To comfort the sorrowing,
   To bear wrongs patiently,
   To forgive wrongs,
   To pray for the living and the dead.

8. Because they wanted to show God how much they loved Him by working for Him alone.

*Teacher's References:*

*Church History,* "St. Francis of Assisi," pages 363–368.

*Catholic School Journal,* "St. Francis and the Birds," March, 1934.

*The Life of the Church,* "St. Francis," pages 186–191.

*Teacher's Notes:*

### Lesson 21

*Aim:* To learn from the lesson of St. Dominic how he obtained the special help of the Blessed Virgin in his fight to save the members of the Mystical Body from being lost to the Church; also the value of the rosary, and how to understand and appreciate it better.

*Preparation:* Review the work of St. Francis and his Order for the Church. At the same time, another saint gathered a number of men around him to do a similar work. It was the great St. Dominic.

### Read Lesson 21

Let the picture aid you in developing the story after the first reading.

Note what traits of character showed themselves even in Dominic's youth.

Show what part of the Dominican habit is known as a scapular.

### Practical Application

Make this a "Rosary Week." Have as many pictures as possible pertaining to the mysteries of the rosary. Have posted on the bulletin board pictures of Dominican saints, also poems and other clippings pertaining to the rosary.

Take this opportunity to make sure that the children understand and know how to say the rosary.

*Things to Do:*

1. St. Dominic, August 4.

2. St. Catherine of Siena, April 30; St. Rose of Lima, August 30.

3. St. Albert the Great, canonized December 16, 1931, and given the title "Doctor of the Church."

4. This activity may take the form of a "Program" with hymns between the stories of each mystery, posters in the form of banners, poems, etc.

5. *Gregory Hymnal,* No. 86, or any other.

6. October 7.

7. Rosary beads are effectively made by using the circles made by a paper punch. Silver or gold beads on a black background is particularly effective.

*Can You Answer These Questions?*

1. Because he knew that the soul is more important than the body. He knew that if a soul is lost it goes to hell and he also knew that Christ gave His life to save souls.

2. We should take greater care of the soul than of the body.

3. The souls of those who die in mortal sin go to hell.

4. Hell is a place of "unquenchable fire" where there is "weeping and gnashing of teeth" as Jesus Himself has said.

5. Make an act of contrition and go to confession as soon as possible.

6. Fed the hungry,
   Clothed the naked,
   Warned sinners,
   Instructed the ignorant,
   Etc.

7. We say the rosary in honor of the Blessed Virgin Mary.

8. The mysteries of the rosary are:
   *Joyful Mysteries:*
      The Annunciation
      The Visitation

The Birth of Jesus in Bethlehem

The Presentation of Jesus in the Temple

The Finding of Jesus in the Temple

*Sorrowful Mysteries:*

The Agony in the Garden

The Scourging

The Crowning with thorns

The Carrying of the cross

The Crucifixion

*The Glorious Mysteries:*

The Resurrection of our Lord from the dead

The Ascension into heaven

The Descent of the Holy Ghost

The Assumption of the Blessed Virgin Mary

The Coronation of the Blessed Virgin Mary

9. Tell the story of each mystery in a few sentences.

**Teacher's References:**

*Church History,* "St. Dominic and the Preaching Friars," pages 361–363.

*Catholic School Journal,* "A Rosary Pageant," October, 1933.

**Teacher's Notes:**

## Lesson 22

*Aim:* To learn the part which St. Thomas Aquinas played in aiding the Church by his wonderful writings.

*Preparation:* The following translations of the *O Salutaris* and *Tantum Ergo* should be read and simplified for the children by the teacher:

### O SALUTARIS

O Saving Victim! opening wide
The Gate of Heaven to man below!
Our foes press on from every side;
Thine aid supply, Thy strength bestow.

To Thy great Name be endless praise,
Immortal Godhead! One in Three!
O grant us endless length of days
In our true native land with thee. Amen.

### TANTUM ERGO

Down in adoration falling
Lo! the sacred Host we hail!
Lo! o'er ancient forms departing,
Newer rites of grace prevail;
Faith for all defects supplying
Where the feeble senses fail.

To the Everlasting Father
And the Son, who reigns on high,
With the Holy Ghost, proceeding
Forth from each eternally,
Be salvation, honor, blessing,
Might and endless majesty.    Amen.

There are many beautiful poems and pictures that will help to make the lesson more impressive. A Blessed Sacrament program could terminate the lesson.

*Holy Viaticum:* Holy Communion at the time of death.

The Church needs all kinds of people to do her work. So far we have read of men who founded religious Orders to preach and teach. Today we shall read of a learned and holy monk whose work was to help others by means of his wonderful writings.

*Read Lesson 22*

What other saint was opposed by his family for becoming a religious? The work of God is not easy. It is full of difficulties. But, what a wonderful reward was that of St. Thomas.

Explain: "The victory Thomas won over evil" — he refused to commit a mortal sin.

Use the picture to repeat the story.

*Practical Application*

Devotion to the Blessed Sacrament should be especially fostered during the week, through the hymns of St. Thomas Aquinas. Hymns in honor of the Blessed Sacrament should be sung frequently and children encouraged to visit the Blessed Sacrament all by themselves to have a little talk with Jesus.

Try to help pupils form habits of thinking good and beautiful thoughts. Be specific in suggesting remedies for evil thoughts. A suitable ejaculation such as "O Mary, conceived without sin, pray for us who have recourse to thee" or "My Jesus, mercy," should be taught.

Stress again and again throughout the year, that we are children of God and that He sees and knows all our thoughts, words, and actions.

*Things to Do:*

3. The Latin words are put into the text because they are usually sung in that language. Check up on the correct pronunciation of the words at this time.

4. March 7, vestment white.

5. The feast occurs on Thursday after Trinity Sunday.

6. It will be necessary to keep the idea of a general council in mind, since it will recur again in later lessons.

7. Words of St. Thomas, the Apostle, "My Lord and my God!"

*Can You Answer These Questions?*

1. St. Thomas is called the "Angelic Doctor" because he was so pure and more like an angel than like a man.

2. The Blessed Sacrament is the Body and Blood of our Lord Jesus Christ.

3. Jesus Christ instituted the Blessed Sacrament.

4. At the Last Supper.

5. Holy Communion received for the last time before death.

6. Against the Sixth Commandment.

7. We must pray, leave the place of temptation, if possible, change one's occupation if that is the cause (for example, reading).

8. Yes, one can also commit sins of thought.

9. God knows whether we are committing such sins.

10. No, they are an approximate occasion of sin.

11. To keep the heart pure we should
    a) pray,
    b) go to the sacraments often,
    c) keep away from bad companions, books, shows, etc.,
    d) try never to be idle but to keep busy doing something all the time.

## Return to Introduction to This Unit:

As a final summary or clinching or organization of this unit, return to its introductory statement and read it again and discuss in the light of all the material of the unit.

## Teacher's References:

*St. Thomas Aquinas* (for children) Maritain (Sheed and Ward).

*Church History,* St. Thomas Aquinas, pages 378–380.

*The Life of the Church,* "Scholasticism — St. Thomas Aquinas," pages 193–199.

## Test Yourself:

These truths should be thoroughly reviewed and, if necessary, explained, until all know and understand them.

1. Mystery.
2. Holy Ghost.
3. Jesus Christ, or God the Son.
4. God the Father.
5. God.
6. Body and soul.
7. God.
8. Apostles' Creed.
9. Body, soul.

10. Body, soul.
11. Soul.
12. Spirit.
13. First.
14. Original.
15. Baptism.

16. Adam and Eve.
17. Redeemer.
18. Jesus.
19. Christmas.
20. Mary.
21. St. Joseph.

*Teacher's Notes:*

# UNIT VII

# THE GREAT REVOLUTION

*Time:* January, third and fourth weeks.

## Feasts to Remember

January  *17   St. Anthony, Abbot
                (Lesson 11.)
        18   Chair of St. Peter
                (Sing the Hymn for the Pope.)
       21   St. Agnes, Martyr
                (Have the pupils tell the story of her life.)
     *24   St. Timothy
                (Lesson 6.)
     *25   Conversion of St. Paul
                (Lesson 5. Call for the quotation on page 33.)
     *29   St. Francis de Sales
                (Lesson 38.)

## *The Unit Introduction:*

Since the children are too young to grasp the full significance of the Reformation, the introduction merely outlines very simply the whole situation, so as to give them at least some little insight into the difficulties the Church had to contend with. In *Religion in Life Curriculum,* which is a part of this series, read "Point of View" on pages 74 and 75. The quotation will help you to know what to stress in this and other lessons.

There is no need of going into detail, of course, but the children should be made to understand something of the significance of the whole movement for our own times. It was at the time of the Great Revolution that the terrible bigotry and hatred against Catholics began.

As in other units, review the introduction after having read the stories, in order the more clearly to see the whole.

### Lesson 23

*Aim:* To show how God inspired St. Ignatius to become an officer in His spiritual army and how this saint became the founder of a great Order of men who fought to win souls for the Church particularly during the time of the Great Revolution, and ever since.

*Preparation:* Look over "Things to Do" and make all your plans ahead of time.

Words to explain:

*Shattered:* broken in several places.

*Faithless:* disloyal, untrue.

Again the popes needed help, this time to preach against the errors of the Great Revolution. Again God raised up saintly men to work for His cause.

### Read Lesson 23

Talk about the lesson in detail. Ignatius Loyola was touched by the *Lives of the Saints;* Francis Xavier, by words from Scripture. What other saint changed his whole life on hearing a certain sentence from Scripture? Good reading has a lasting influence on our lives.

Make this a Catholic Literature Week or plan on having such a week sometime during February, Catholic Press Month. If possible, let it embrace all Catholic literature from first to fifth grades and invite the other classes to co-operate.

### Ask Yourself:

If the children are not in the habit of reading religious books suitable for their age, perhaps you can seize this occasion to interest them in such reading. Make sure, to begin with, that the books you offer them are really interesting. The *Medal Stories,* for example, are excellent reading. See also list of Children's books, page 193. Perhaps this would be a chance to obtain religious books suitable for your grade. There is no longer any reason for saying that children do not like to read books pertaining to religious subjects. Children will read anything that arouses their interest. Strive to cultivate their taste gradually for things spiritual. It can be done by giving them for appreciation, stories, poems, and other selections of a spiritual nature and by showing a wholehearted enthusiasm for them yourself. Almost every lesson in this book aims at that very thing. But the teacher must remember that her own attitude is the biggest factor in bringing about the desired results.

*Things to Do:*

1. You might remark incidentally that *The Lives of the Saints* should be in every good Catholic home. The thought may bear fruit in later years. Recall what this book did for St. Ignatius. It may do something similar for others who read it.

(The teacher can also influence parents to select the right kind of gift books for their children. Her apostolic work in this respect may have far-reaching results.)

2. Use these compositions for booklets or readings during your Catholic literature program.

3. This, too, might be included in the program.

4. A person's favorite magazine will tell a great deal about his taste. Watch the result. Do not insist, however, for there may be no good magazines at home, or the child may bring one out of a sense of duty and not as a matter of taste.

5. Interest pupils in worth-while periodicals or magazines.

*The Young Catholic Messenger*    *The Manna*
*The Schoolmate*
*The Little Missionary*

6. Carry this out by all means unless the pupils in your school are already well equipped in this regard. This gives you a splendid

opportunity to interest the children in good books and periodicals. The interest of the P.T.A. or Catholic School and Home Association could be enlisted.

7. Posters should be used for different phases of the exhibit.

8. Aim to make these talks an outgrowth of the pupils' own convictions.

9. Notice the significance of the motto for parents also.

10. Let the pupils have the pleasure of making their own suggestions. Afterwards help them choose the best ways. Where there is no Catholic literature in the home, let the pupils take home papers or magazines brought by others and leave them, with other reading material, without comment.

Street cars, railroad stations, doctors' offices, etc., are good places in which to *forget* a Catholic paper, or magazine. Do not undertake a great deal. Getting good reading into their own homes or passing it on for others is a good start for the children. Watch for requests for Catholic literature in Catholic periodicals and at least call the pupils' attention to the need.

11. If it is not possible for individuals to get the magazines mentioned, perhaps the class as a whole could get them.

12. The teacher will have to decide the best place to send Catholic literature. There is much to be done in this regard. Start the children now in their concern for other people's souls.

13. Stop to make the good intention with the children at times, and again remind them to make it quietly.

In keeping with our aim to have children *live* their religion, it is well to remember that we should leave many practices to the individual rather than to the group. Too many prayers and religious practices done wholesale and in a group are not conducive to the formation of personal habits of piety.

*Can You Answer These Questions?*

1. Obey the Commandments of God and of the Church and do all our duties the very best we can.

2. Through mortal sin.

3. The loss of sanctifying grace through mortal sin.

4. Baptism and penance.

5. Baptism takes away all sin from the soul, makes us Christians, children of God and heirs of heaven. It also takes away the temporal and eternal punishment due to sin.

6. Yes, if we read something against faith or against purity and we keep on reading it just because it gives us pleasure or we want to do it, we sin.

7. If a book or magazine causes us to doubt our faith or leads us into other temptations, we know that we should not read it.

8. Put the book away at once and start doing something else.

9. Scandal.

10. By bad example and by evil advice or suggestion.

*Teacher's References:*

*Church History,* "St. Ignatius Loyola and the Society of Jesus," pages 461–465.

*The Life of the Church,* "The Reformation," Chap. VIII; "St. Ignatius Loyola," pages 232–238.

*Catholic Action Series,* Book III, "The Library of the Catholic Home," page 90; "The Catholic Home and Newspapers," page 91; "Reading," page 385.

*Journal of Religious Instruction,* editorial "In Anticipation of Catholic Press Month," November, 1933.

*Catholic School Journal,* "The Book House," June, 1934.

*Teacher's Notes:*

## Lesson 24

*Aim:* To learn how the Church, through the Council of Trent, healed the wounds made by her unfaithful children during the Great Revolution.

*Preparation:* Recall what a general council is, and by what other name it may be called. The lesson will require careful preparation, so that every point can be clearly and very simply presented to the children.

### Read Lesson 24

You will have to go over each paragraph slowly and carefully, making sure that the pupils get the general outlines correct. Do not enter into detailed explanations but aim at a clear understanding of the statements made in the text.

Have the children look back and see when the Lateran Palace was mentioned before.

### Practical Application

1. There are seven sacraments: Baptism, Confirmation, Holy Eucharist, Penance, Extreme Unction, Holy Orders, Matrimony.

2. Baptism, confirmation, and Holy Orders.

3. Baptism and penance (sacraments of the dead).

4. Holy Orders.

5. Baptism.

6. Confirmation, Holy Eucharist, Extreme Unction, Holy Orders, Matrimony (sacraments of the living).

7. Extreme Unction.

8. Baptism.

9. It is the unbloody renewal of the Sacrifice of the Cross.

10. Because they owe worship to God their Creator and the Church commands that they hear Mass every Sunday and holyday of obligation.

11. Jesus said the first Mass at the Last Supper.

12. The Poor Souls are the souls of those who died without mortal sin on their souls but cannot enter heaven until they are entirely purified from sin.

13. Pray, have Masses said, do penance and good works, gain indulgences for them.

14. They cannot commit sin.

15. They cannot be lost because they can no longer commit sin.

16. Jesus Christ.

17. Pope Pius XI.

18. In Rome, in Vatican City, a part of Rome.

19. Yes, just as any other person.

20. Yes, just as we do.

21. To any priest he may choose.

22. No. He tells us only what we must believe in regard to faith and morals. He also advises Catholics sometimes, but he does not meddle in politics.

**Return to Introduction to This Unit:**

As a final summary or clinching or organization of this unit, return to its introductory statement and read it again and discuss in the light of all the material of the unit.

**Teacher's References:**

*Church History*, "The Council of Trent," pages 477–480.

*Catholic Action Series,* Book III, "Catholic Education," page 104.

*The Life of the Church,* "The Catholic Awakening," pages 227–232.

*Teacher's Notes:*

# UNIT VIII

# THE CHURCH, MOTHER OF ART AND LEARNING

*Time:* February.

## Feasts to Remember

February    2  Candlemas
(Sing a hymn in honor of Mary. Also let one or the other pupil read or recite a poem to Mary.)

        3  St. Blase

    *6  St. Dorothy
(The little episode of the basket of fruit and flowers would make a beautiful dramatization for this feast.)

  *10  St. Scholastica
(Sister of St. Benedict.)

  *11  Our Lady of Lourdes
(Sing a hymn to Mary. Have the children tell the story of Our Lady of Lourdes, if they can get it from another book. See also references for Lesson 35.)

   22  St. Peter's Chair at Antioch
(Sing the Hymn for the Pope.)

  *24  St. Matthias, Apostle
(Was chosen in place of Judas. Have the pupils find what he did for the Church and how he died.)

## The Unit Introduction:

Try to give the pupils some understanding of the spirit of faith that characterized the Middle Ages. Do not go too much into detail, but rather aim to give a good general picture and to make clear the statements in the text. Faith animated all the works of the people. All this began with the conversion of the pagans, therefore long before the Great Revolution. All Christian people realized that they were children of God and they tried to express their faith and piety in many ways. The result was some of the greatest masterpieces the world possesses today.

When you read this introduction again at the end of the month, use it as a review of the unit by asking for specific examples relating to the general statements made. For example, the statement "There were great schools and universities" would call for the question: "What schools and universities were mentioned in the text?"

### Lesson 25

*Aim:* To understand from her history why the Church can truly be called the Mother of Learning.

*Preparation:* If possible, have on hand pictures of the early monastery schools and monastery workshops. Use this week also to teach more about your own school, stressing in particular the sacrifices made by those dedicated to the service of God and also by parents to maintain Catholic schools.

There is much opportunity for a correlation of religion and life. Children of a Catholic school should be deeply imbued with the thought that all their thoughts, words, and actions are known to God and should be becoming of a child of God. In view of all the historical and religious facts they have gathered, it becomes almost self-evident that the Catholic school is the only school for them.

*Read Lesson 25*

Recall the famous teachers of Charlemagne's time. Look at the picture on page 148 and talk about it. Explain that the word *manuscript* means "written by hand." Some of these old Bibles and other manuscripts are preserved in libraries and museums with great care. If you can obtain rare books or manuscripts or visit a library where such can be seen, you will give the children valuable training in appreciation.

Recall also what has been read about St. Albert the Great and St. Thomas Aquinas.

*Things to Do:*

A project on "My Parish School" would help to focus interest in your own school. In that case be sure to tie up the early history of church schools with it; that is, show by some reading such as this lesson and the following, that the Church is the mother of all learning.

*Can You Answer These Questions?*

1. By listening to the instructions of their parents, pastors, and teachers and by attending a Catholic school.

2. Because they are in the world to know, and love, and serve God, which is what religion really means; and they must learn these things from those whom God has given authority over them.

3. The Fourth Commandment.

4. Pastors, teachers, and those who govern the state and country.

5. This question should bring out by discussion how a sincere Catholic must always live according to the dictates of his conscience. Also, it may help to develop a good class and school spirit.

*Teacher's References:*

*Church History,* "The Carolingian Revival of Learning," pages 256–258; "Rise of the Medieval Universities," pages 372–377.

*A Book of Religion for Elementary Schools,* "Writing Room of a Monastery" (picture), page 259.

*Teacher's Notes:*

## Lesson 26

*Aim:* To learn from the story of St. John Baptist de la Salle how a new Order of teachers was founded to continue more effectively the work of the Church as the teacher of all her children.

*Preparation:* Read carefully the activities proposed and make your plans according to the needs of your own class.

In every age God called up saints who recognized the particular needs of the times and gave freely of their services for the Church. Such a saint was John Baptist de la Salle. We shall see in our story how much Catholics of today owe to this saint.

*Read Lesson 26*

Have the children point out the outstanding characteristics of St. John de la Salle as they are revealed from paragraph to paragraph. It is such generous souls that God makes use of in particular to carry on His work.

*Practical Application*

Be careful, in dealing with the problems, not to make a sin of every thoughtless act. The point is chiefly to make the children aware of their gifts and their duties.

You can do much good here by pointing out that all normal people can learn to do one or the other thing well. The fact that one child has great talent for study and another not, does not mean that the other has no particular aptitude. He may be able to draw well, to construct an engine, and so on. Try to give the children of meager talent confidence in themselves and to get them over the idea that they are of no particular use.

1. Bring out here the fact that when God gives a child talent for study, He expects him to make use of it.

2. Health is a splendid gift of God. We may not squander it according to our own feelings.

3. Nellie is wasting money. She has a duty to perform in obedience to her mother, even if she is not particularly talented. You might dwell on the pleasure it gives the mother to hear Nellie play and to know that she will be able to perform on the piano.

4. The two boys are squandering precious time not only for themselves but for all whom they disturb. Again be careful to point out the good they could accomplish and their duty to make proper use of time rather than to be too specific or severe about the fault.

5. Anna can explain the work to him and help him understand his work, since God has given her that particular talent. She should not do his homework for him.

6. Mert ought to be happy to use his particular talent to give others pleasure, even if he has to make extra sacrifices. That would be one way of showing God gratitude for the gift.

7. Discuss practical ways of making one's self useful. Della should do all in her power to make grandfather happy. She might bring him his pipe, read or sing to him, prepare or help him prepare the meals, surprise him with some favorite dish or a bunch of flowers, etc.

8. Discuss how we must co-operate in order to do things worth while. If there is to be a band, someone has to make sacrifices to have a good band. How about Father Lord and the rest? Boys and girls who never give up their own time for others, become very selfish, and no one loves a selfish person.

9. Teach here the care of personal belongings, even supposing no one else notices or cares. For two reasons Jamie should get the book. First of all, it is worth money and secondly it represents the love of another person for him. By not caring for it, he shows that he does not know the value of either.

10. Responsibility for the things we get and have charge of should be pointed out here. It is not so much the seed we should think of, as the character trait reliability, that needs looking after.

### Things to Do:

1. Notice particularly the cathedral, but do not dwell on it too long at this time. Lesson 29 develops Gothic architecture.

5. Charity, generosity.

7. It is well to dramatize some of these little actions until they become familiar.

### Can You Answer These Questions?

1. The priesthood.

2. Holy Orders.

3. An indelible mark as does baptism and confirmation.

4. The sacrifice of the Mass.

5. The Mass is the unbloody renewal of the Sacrifice of the Cross.

6. A sacrifice is the offering to God of a visible gift, whole and entire.

7. Christ offers Himself again at Mass the same as He did on Calvary.

8. On Calvary He shed His blood and at Mass He does not.

9. We should hear Mass with attention and devotion.

10. Every Sunday and holyday of obligation.

11. January 1, Circumcision of our Lord; Forty Days after Easter, Ascension of our Lord; August 15, Assumption of the Blessed Virgin Mary; November 1, All Saints; December 8, Immaculate Conception; December 25, Christmas.

12. The Third Commandment.

13. We may not do servile work.

*Teacher's References:*

*Catholic Action Series,* Book I, Holy Orders, pages 227–233; Book III, "Eight Steps to a Worthy Vocational Life," page 156; "Opportunities for Catholic Action," pages 156–163.

*Teacher's Notes:*

## Lesson 27

*Aim:* To learn from the story of Michelangelo how the people of the Middle Ages expressed their faith through the great works of art.

*Preparation:* Have pictures of Michelangelo, statue of David, the statue of Moses, of the Pieta, and any other pictures pertaining to the lesson.

Words to explain:

*Sculpture:* the art of carving in stone.

*Faun:* a woodland god who helps farmers and shepherds. "A faun was thought to look like a man but had the ears, horns, tail, and sometimes the legs of a goat." *Thorndike Century Junior Dictionary.*

*Chisel:* a sharp instrument used by a sculptor to carve stone.

*Architect:* one who makes the plans for the construction of buildings.

An important point to stress in this and the two following lessons is the fact that it was the popes who were the principal patrons of art. But for their support much of the great work of the Middle Ages could not have been accomplished. Also, it was religion that furnished inspiration for practically all the great masterpieces of literature, painting, sculpture, and architecture. For that reason we can truly say that the Church is the Mother of Art. In this lesson we shall learn about the greatest sculptor that lived in the Middle Ages.

*Read Lesson 27*

*Explain:* "A whole world of art seemed to open before him" — in his mind he seemed to see what wonderful things might be done in marble.

"Give me a mountain to carve" — give me some big blocks of marble to carve statues from.

Michelangelo loved to read the Bible. The greatest artists of the Middle Ages found their inspiration in the stories of the Bible. That is why so many masterpieces picture Biblical scenes and characteristics.

Discuss the saying of Michelangelo.

*Ask Yourself:*

Be specific in your application of these questions. Let each pupil choose one thing he can improve upon and carry out the resolution as soon as possible.

*Things to Do:*

Seize every opportunity possible to have the pupils read and relate Old Testament stories.

If the pupils do any carving, do not lose sight of the fact that it should aid them in learning something about the art and especially in appreciating more fully the work of the great sculptors.

Michelangelo painted pictures of stories from the Book of Genesis to the Flood.

*Can You Answer These Questions?*

1. Mary is called the Sorrowful Mother because she is said to have been pierced by seven great sorrows as with a sword. Feast of the Sorrowful Mother, Passion Week, and September 15.

2. *a*) The prophecy of Simeon.
   *b*) The loss of Jesus for three days.
   *c*) Flight into Egypt.
   *d*) The meeting of Jesus on the way to Calvary.
   *e*) The death of Jesus on the cross.
   *g*) Jesus is laid in the arms of His Mother.
   *h*) The burial of Jesus.

3. The Agony in the Garden.
   The Scourging.
   The Crowning with Thorns.
   The Carrying of the Cross.
   The Crucifixion.

4. Christ died to redeem us from the consequences of original sin and all other sins and to gain heaven for us.

5. He remained in the grave three days.

6. In Limbo.

7. Limbo is a place of rest where the souls of the just were

waiting for Christ to come and take them to heaven with Him.

8. On Easter Day.

9. Yes, there are pagans who adore idols today.

10. Superstition is the attributing to things a strange hidden power which God has not given to them.

11. Friday the 13th an unlucky day; A horseshoe bringing good luck; a broken mirror, seven years bad luck, etc.

*Teacher's References:*

*Church History,* "The Popes as Patrons of Art," pages 413–418.

*Catholic Action Series,* Book III, "Art as a Career," pages 464–465.

*Teacher's Notes:*

## Lesson 28

*Aim:* To learn about the great artist Raphael and his wonderful religious paintings, produced during the Middle Ages.

*Preparation:* Gather as many pictures as you possibly can of Raphael's Madonnas. The Public Library may be able to help you.

Do all in your power to teach appreciation of true art especially of the great religious art which cannot be surpassed.

Explain that a legend is a story from the past which many people have believed, but which is not historical.

Keep in mind that we are dealing with the spirit of faith manifested in the Middle Ages in so many beautiful ways. We have heard about the Church schools. We have learned about Michelangelo's great statues. We shall now hear of an artist whose great devotion to Christian art produced the most splendid paintings that the world has ever seen.

*Read Lesson 28*

Discuss the lesson in detail.

In addition to the picture in the book, have on hand ready for discussion the *Madonna della Sedia* (Madonna of the Chair). Talk about the two pictures at length, pointing out that only a soul filled with love for the Madonna could produce anything so beautiful.

Notice that Raphael, too, derived much of his inspiration from the Bible.

*Practical Application*

Encourage the children to treasure the best known of Raphael's pictures.

Sing a hymn to Mary every day and if possible learn a new one in her honor.

Let the pupils write compositions about Madonna pictures and also original poems and prayers in her honor.

A little Madonna Booklet with the Madonna of the Chair on the cover would make a suitable program or souvenir for each child.

An additional activity would be to have the pupils look for all the different feasts of the Blessed Virgin Mary on the calendar.

The suggested program should not represent special work but rather be a review of the best selections, hymns, compositions, etc., of the week.

*Can You Answer These Questions?*

1. The Blessed Virgin Mary is the Mother of God.

2. Jesus Christ became man by coming down from heaven to be born of the Blessed Virgin Mary.

3. He was born on Christmas Day.

4. He became man to redeem us.

5. Jesus Christ was always God with the Father and the Holy Ghost.

6. He is true God because He Himself said so, because He showed it by His miracles, and because in Him all the Scriptures were fulfilled.

7. There are two natures in Jesus Christ, the human and the divine.

8. There is only one person in Jesus Christ, the divine.

*Teacher's References:*

*Catholic Encyclopedia,* "Raphael Santi."

*Catholic School Journal,* "Pictures in Religious Instruction," July, 1934; "The Story of Medieval Art," January, 1934.

*Teacher's Notes:*

## Lesson 29

*Aim:* To learn from a study of the great Gothic cathedrals something of the spirit of living faith that expressed itself in such glorious monuments during the Middle Ages; and, to cultivate a just pride in these great works.

*Preparation:* Have on hand as many pictures of the great Gothic cathedrals as possible. Include also pictures of beautiful church windows and other religious ornaments and symbols. (If you can get old copies of the *Catholic Directory,* you will find much material in the advertisements.)

If you wish to carry out the theme in a larger way, posters, compositions, etc., may appear in church-window designs. They are easily made and very effective. Colored paper from the inside of envelopes, cellophane, and other brilliant papers make an excellent background.

Look over the entire lesson and map out your work ahead of time.

The Catholic schools very often lack the beautiful furnishings, grand gymnasiums, swimming pools, etc., which are the boast of the public schools. Nevertheless, Catholics have in their possession so many more precious things; their great churches, in which reposes the Blessed Sacrament; their wonderful works of art, etc. Try to fill the children with a just pride in the possession of these treasures. Naturally that will mean a keen appreciation on your part, for "We cannot give what we do not possess."

### Read Lesson 29

Develop each paragraph more fully. The first paragraph shows the spirit that prompted the erection of the great Gothic cathedrals.

The second paragraph states the time and manner in which the work was carried out. It might be of interest to name the persons that lived and the events that took place during this time; that is, between the eleventh and fifteenth centuries.

The third paragraph shows the extensive use of symbols and the reason for their use. All are creatures of God. All should honor Him! Plants, such as grapes, wheat, the lilies, etc.; animals, such as the dove, representing the Holy Ghost and often the soul; the thirsty hart, drinking from the fountain as the thirsty soul drinks of the Blood of Christ, etc.

### Practical Application

Take this opportunity to remind the children that prayer is talking to God. Surely, when we talk to God we ought not just to say words that we do not mean.

### Things to Do:

1. This should make an interesting written or oral language lesson.

2. Teach the simpler symbols, such as the following: Cross, crown, palm, keys, grapes, wheat, lily, lamb, IHS, M, PX. Recall what the lesson says about them.

3. Note the reference to the *Shield's Religion Book*. It has splendid material.

4. If you prefer, you might call attention to some local church instead.

5, 6. Another exercise for the language period.

7. Be sure to recall the meaning of gargoyles on the great Gothic cathedrals, as stated in the text.

8. Just before the preface.

9. If this can be made a class excursion, so much the better.

10. Be sure to use the quotations again whenever possible.

*Can You Answer These Questions?*

1. Because they knew they serve as the house of God.

2. The sacrifice of the Mass.

3. Prayer is a lifting up of the heart and mind to God.

4. We should pray:

    *a*) With attention;

    *b*) With the thought that we of our own accord can do nothing and God can do everything;

    *c*) With a great desire to obtain what we ask for;

    *d*) With trust in God's goodness;

    *e*) With perseverance.

5. See text, page 176.

6. We always receive an answer to our prayers, but not always in the way in which we expect it.

7. The Lord's Prayer, the Hail Mary, the Apostles' Creed, Acts of faith, hope, and charity, Act of contrition, etc.

8. The Our Father or the Lord's Prayer.

9. A symbol is an emblem or sign that stands for or represents something else.

10. The dove represents the Holy Ghost; the IHS, the Redeemer of mankind; the PX, Christ; the crossed keys, the authority of the Church; the lamb, Christ, the Lamb of God; etc.

*Return to Introduction to This Unit:*

As a final summary or clinching or organization of this unit, return to its introductory statement and read it again and discuss in the light of all the material of the unit.

*Teacher's References:*

*Church History*, "Medieval Architecture," pages 386–388.

*A Book of Religion for Elementary Schools*, "Gothic Cathedrals," page 265.

*Catholic School Journal,* "Symbolism in Ecclesiastical Art,"
June, 1934; "Color in Symbolism," November, 1934; "Symbols,"
December, 1934.

*The Life of the Church,* "Development of the Externals of
Religion," pages 174–180.

*Test Yourself:*

1. Charlemagne.
2. Mohammed.
3. Crusades.
4. Cross.
5. Palestine.
6. God wills it.
7. Henry IV.
8. Hospital.
9. Crusade.
10. Franciscan.
11. Rosary.
12. Blessed Sacrament.
13. Jesus.
14. Monk.
15. Michelangelo.
16. Popes.
17. Vatican.
18. Cathedrals, Gothic.
19. Religion.
20. Universities.

*Teacher's Notes:*

*Teacher's Notes:*

# UNIT IX

## THE CHURCH AND THE NATIONS

*Time:* March.

### Feasts to Remember

March  *7  St. Thomas Aquinas
            (Lesson 22. Review the story and sing one of the hymns written by St. Thomas.)

      *17  St. Patrick
            (Lesson 30. Have a program in honor of St. Patrick.)

       19  St. Joseph, Patron of the Universal Church. (Sing a hymn or read a poem in honor of the Saint. Show how fitting it is that he who cared for the Saviour on earth should also be made the special protector of His Church.)

      *21  St. Benedict
            (Review Lesson 12.)

       24  St. Gabriel, Archangel

       25  Annunciation
            (Connect the story of the feast with the prayer "Hail Mary" and use this occasion to renew the children's fervor in reciting the prayer.)

### The Unit Introduction:

Use this occasion once more to give a unified general picture of the work of the Church through her great leaders.

When the lessons have been completed, review these paragraphs by recalling the names of the missionaries mentioned, the age in which they labored, and the countries they helped to convert. Then read the introduction once more, to summarize the work of the unit.

## Lesson 30

*Aim:* To learn how St. Patrick brought the Faith to Ireland and how it spread from there to other countries.

*Preparation:* Since the Feast of St. Patrick will be celebrated soon, you might plan ahead and use this week's work as a preparation for the day's celebration, if there is to be any.

For yourself read over Lesson 42 so that you may keep in mind the connection between the two stories and aim at preparing the way for Lesson 42.

Have ready the two poems "Shield of St. Patrick" and "Kindness is the Word" (reading list). They could be posted on the bulletin board ahead of time. Recall to the children the words with which Christ bade the Apostles go out and teach all nations. (Matt. xxviii. 19.)

*Read Lesson 30*

Stress in particular the fact that the Island brought forth many great missionaries who later helped to convert other nations; also the strong faith of the people which could not be extinguished through centuries of hardship and persecution.

Explain any terms that the children may not fully understand. What, for example, would be understood by "the corporal and spiritual ills of his children"?

*Ask Yourself:*

Suggest specific acts of kindness that may be performed in each place mentioned.

It is important to teach the children just how they can go about their evening examination of conscience and to have them cultivate a habit of making a daily examination. Use a little dramatization for the purpose. In asking himself about this particular act of kindness for the day, added to his examination of conscience a boy might say: "Did I keep my resolution to do a kind act? No, I forgot. Dear God, I meant to do an act of kindness to one of the boys in school today and I forgot all about it. I am ashamed of myself. You think of me all the time, dear God, and do so much for me, and here I forget even one little resolution. Please forgive me. I will try again tomorrow," or: "Dear God, I thought of my little act of kindness today. It was fun doing it for You and it made me happy, too. I am going to try to do more like that every day for You. Thank You, dear God, for helping me."

*Things to Do:*

Work of this kind may be varied from week to week. The lives of the saints may be used for oral talks, written composition, dramatization, etc.

3. St. Columba or Columkille, June 9, Apostle of the Picts in Scotland.

4. See "The Lion and the Slave," *De La Salle Reader,* Book IV, page 29.

Such acts may well be dramatized in a very simple way, principally to bring to the children's minds the many little acts of kindness they can do.

5. A few important truths about the Trinity may be brought into the dialog in order to make it more instructive for the class.

6. Any other suitable St. Patrick poem or prayer may be substituted.

8. Add other Bible stories showing kindness, such as the story of the Good Samaritan. It is well to use such stories occasionally. Different members of the class might be appointed to tell different stories.

9. Have a few of the simpler stories related as a whole.

10. Be sure the children get the application of this text.

12. Use these texts frequently.

*Can You Answer These Questions?*

1. Holy Orders.

2. By men who have been properly prepared for the holy priesthood.

3. The bishop.

4. An indelible mark; that is, one that can never be effaced.

5. Baptism and Confirmation.

6. Of the Holy Trinity.

7. The great gift of faith (Abraham, an example of faith).

8. In Baptism.

9. Hope and love or charity (Job, an example of hope; Magdalen, an example of love).

10. The acts of faith, hope, and charity.

*Teacher's References:*

*Church History,* "St. Patrick and the Conversion of Ireland," pages 178–182.

*The Life of the Church,* "The Church and the Barbarians," pages 164–165.

*Teacher's Notes:*

## Lesson 31

*Aim:* To learn what the German people owe to St. Boniface and to those who helped him spread the faith in their country.

*Preparation:* Have a picture of the Good Shepherd, also the gospel for the second Sunday after Easter. Jesus called Himself the Good Shepherd who gives His life for His sheep. Many of the apostles of the nations, like their great Leader, also laid down their lives for those whom they were trying to save. Among them was St. Boniface, the Apostle of Germany.

*Read Lesson 31*

Talk about the lesson. Have the children retell the story with the help of the picture.

St. Boniface went to England for volunteer missionaries. In the early days of our country, from what nations did the priests come to convert the Indians?

Today our own boys and girls volunteer to go to other countries to save souls. What countries do they go to?

*Practical Application*

Speak · of the love of the Good Shepherd for us. Try to impress the lesson so deeply upon the children that they will remember it for life. Just as the Good Shepherd willingly gave His life to redeem us, so St. Boniface was willing to give his life for souls. He loves every soul, no matter how sinful, and longs to bring it back to the fold. Every time we go to confession and tell God how sorry we are for our sins, He takes us into His arms and forgives and forgets everything. How good God is!

If you have succeeded in establishing the right atmosphere, have the children rise and fold their hands reverently for prayer. They may pray in some such words as the following: "Dear Jesus, I thank You for Your great love for me. Please keep me always near You. But if I should get lost through mortal sin, please save me. Help me to come back quickly into Your arms."

If desirable, the children could make a little booklet, just a folded paper, bearing the title: "My prayer to Jesus." Let each one write his own little prayer inside and sign his name to it. The aim is to teach the pupils how to talk to the Lord in their own words.

*Things to Do:*

3. Be sure to connect the story with the drawings. A composition telling about the tree or the chapel, could be part of the work.

4. St. Boniface, martyr, red vestment; St. Lioba, virgin, white vestment.

5. Let the children talk about the picture.

7. This is just a little exercise to help establish chronological connections between the stories.

*Can You Answer These Questions?*

1. Confirmation is a sacrament through which we receive the Holy Ghost to make us strong and perfect Christians and soldiers of Jesus Christ.

2. This sacrament may be received only once.

3. The bishop administers Confirmation.

4. In the state of grace; that is, without mortal sin on the soul.

5. By an act of contrition and a good confession.

6. As often as we are truly sorry and ask His forgiveness.

7. God's mercy and long suffering.

8. "Forgive us our trespasses as we forgive those who trespass against us."

9. By dying on the cross for us.

10. Because He loved us and wished to redeem us from the punishments of sin.

11. Because heaven was closed by the sin of our first parents.

12. The sin known as original sin.

*Teacher's References:*

*Church History,* "St. Boniface, the Apostle of Germany," pages 219–230.

*Teacher's Notes:*

## Lesson 32

*Aim:* To learn of the missionary labors of St. Francis Xavier, who made up in the East the loss that the Church was sustaining in the West through the Great Revolution.

*Preparation:* If possible plan to correlate this lesson with the geography of India, China, and Japan.

Have the class read once more the story of St. Ignatius Loyola, in order to get the connection between the two lessons.

*Read Lesson 32*

Talk over the lesson paragraph by paragraph. Find the lesson about St. Paul and locate the words: "I shall show him what great things he must suffer for My name's sake."

Try to infuse something of the burning zeal for souls, which St. Francis had, into the hearts of the children.

*Practical Application*

Perhaps you would like to teach the hymn of St. Francis Xavier, "My God, I love Thee," *O Deus, Ego Amo Te.* You will need to explain some of the lines.

Impress the children with the fact that it is only those who have formed good habits from youth who can hope to do great things in later life. Discuss thoroughly each thought suggested and make specific applications.

*It Takes Courage to Hold On:*

Apply each of these statements to the small incidents of everyday life. Otherwise little will be gained. For example, give a little situation such as the following: Ray gave the wrong answer to Sister's question. He feels ashamed. Someone behind him punches him in the back and says: "Good for you, smarty!" Ray feels like answering back or telling Sister. It takes courage for him to keep still.

*Things to Do:*

1. Establish the time connection between the two stories.

2, 3. The route leads around Africa. There is much opportunity in this lesson for correlation with geography.

4. St. Francis Xavier, December 3, white vestment.

5. Paul, burning with zeal, converting whole nations, traveling on foot almost alone, etc.

Like Moses, Francis was allowed to look at the Promised Land (China) from a distance but could not enter.

6. The Council of Trent opened 1545, closed 1563.

*Can You Answer These Questions?*

1. "What doth it profit a man if he gain the whole world but suffer the loss of his soul?"

2. What good does it do a person to work for riches and honors if he forgets about God and loses his soul?

3. Idolatry is giving to a creature the honor which belongs to God alone.

4. The First Commandment.

5. (The following definition should be explained by the teacher.) A miracle is an extraordinary event, perceptible to the senses, which exceeds the known powers of nature, and can be traced to a divine cause.

6. Yes, God still works miracles.

7. The miracles at Lourdes.

8. The man who believes something simply because God or the Church said it, shows that he has that true faith which Jesus so often praised in the Gospels.

*Teacher's References:*

*Church History,* "St. Francis Xavier," pages 465–466.

*Catholic Action Series:* Book III, "The Spirit of the World and the Spirit of Christ," pages 43–45.

*Teacher's Notes:*

## Lesson 33

*Aim:* To learn how the Church spread to the New World through the work of zealous missionaries.

*Preparation:* Establish historical connection between this and other lessons. The great Protestant Revolution started in 1517. Compare that date with the birth of Francis Xavier and the other missionaries, and with the discovery of America, 1492.

Recall that in the life of St. Ignatius Loyola it was mentioned that the Church was gaining in pagan countries what she was losing from her own fold through the Protestant Revolution. The story of today shows us what heroic work the missionaries did in the New World.

*Read Lesson 33*

As the children repeat the story paragraph by paragraph, take time to bring in examples and incidents from the past, to illustrate the statements as they are reviewed. For example, in paragraph one, recall how the Church had its beginning in Jerusalem and then spread to Rome. In paragraph two we are reminded of the spirit of the Middle Ages. Use the history text to fill in the story of the discovery of America.

Show how greed for gold among the Christian explorers hindered rather than helped the Church. It is the same today. There are wealthy people who use their money for evil instead of good. In that way they help to tear away other souls from God and the Church.

*Practical Application*

In the practical examples, try to bring home to the children the idea that it is a splendid thing to be of service to others. Awaken in the children the desire to learn how to do things for themselves. Perhaps you can give some of the more "helpless" pupils an opportunity to do little things in the classroom with a view to making them helpful and reliable.

Be specific in talking over the suggestions and problems.

The problems offer occasion for little lessons and talks on First Aid and in many other ways. Stress frequently that usefulness does not come with the occasion but by continued practice.

*What Would You Do?*

1. Show by actual example what should be done: to stop the flow of blood, to get help, etc.

2. See what reactions you get from the children. Of course, a child could not judge of the seriousness of a case. A neighbor should be called, if possible; the priest and the doctor, if necessary. The aim is to make the children aware of the various possibilities within their reach.

3. Not by doing the work for him but by helping him understand the lesson better.

4. The first thing Larry should do is to make a good confession. Let the children discuss this situation.

5. Here is another opportunity for a First-Aid Lesson.

6. Jack should convince himself that there is really something wrong and then report the matter at once. The problem should bring out the responsibility and interest of the individual.

7. Call in a neighbor at once. The aim here again is to suggest the right thing to do and the promptness with which it should be done.

8. Let the children suggest various ways of helping their mothers. It may be that just being very quiet is the best and only thing to do.

*Things to Do:*

These activities offer a chance for correlation with American history and geography. Let the children compare dates and facts.

Be sure to explain to the children what a seminary is and give them some idea of the work done there.

*Can You Answer These Questions?*

1. Scandal, injustice, greed, theft, etc.

2. Stealing.

3. Practically all the corporal and spiritual works of mercy. Let the children enumerate.

4. God's own promise to take care of His own, God's goodness, mercy, etc.

5. Against the Sixth Commandment.

6. Impurity in thoughts, words, and actions.

7. By prayer, receiving the sacraments often, keeping away from bad company, books, shows, etc.

8. Against the Eighth Commandment.

9. Against the Fifth Commandment.

*Return to Introduction to This Unit:*

As a final summary or clinching or organization of this unit, return to its introductory statement and read it again and discuss in the light of all the material of the unit.

*Teacher's References:*

*The Life of the Church,* "Foreign Missions," pages 292–295.

*Church History,* "Missions and Missionaries in the New World," pages 467–473.

*Catholic Action Series,* Book I, "Organizations of the Church," pages 13–19.

*A Game with the Saints:*

Answers:

| | |
|---|---|
| 1. St. Patrick | 11. St. Peter Claver |
| 2. St. Rose of Lima | 12. St. Ignatius Loyola |
| 3. St. Boniface | 13. St. Bernard |
| 4. St. Gregory VII | 14. St. Anne |
| 5. St. Turibius | 15. St. Francis Solanus |
| 6. St. Francis Assisi | 16. St. Albert the Great |
| 7. Pope Innocent III | 17. St. John Baptist de la Salle |
| 8. St. Francis Xavier | 18. St. Lioba |
| 9. St. Dominic | 19. St. Louis Bertrand |
| 10. St. Thomas Aquinas | 20. St. Columba |

*Teacher's Notes:*

# UNIT X

## THE CHURCH AS A TEACHER

*Time:* First two weeks of April.

### Feasts to Remember

April *10 St. Bernadette of Lourdes
(See suggestions for Lesson 35 in this manual.)

13 St. Leo the Great, Pope
(Have the pupils find what was his work for the Church.)
Palm Sunday
Maundy Thursday
Good Friday
Holy Saturday
Easter Sunday
(Do not neglect to talk about the more important ceremonies of Holy Week, but keep well within the comprehension of the pupils.)

### *The Unit Introduction:*

Impress upon the children the right of the Church to teach infallible truth. Do not go any further into the subject, but aim rather at a clear explanation of the truths here stated and at a simple acceptance of the Church's teachings.

If there is time, have the children tell the New Testament story containing the quotation mentioned. It may be found in Matt. xxviii.

Review the paragraph as usual, at the close of the two weeks, in order to relate the two lessons more closely with the general thought, "The Church as a Teacher."

## Lesson 34

*Aim:* To learn from the lesson on the Vatican Council how the Church frequently makes use of the authority to teach, which Christ Himself has given her.

*Preparation:* Keep in mind that it was at this time in particular that men questioned the teaching authority of the pope and the Church.

As an approach to the story review the lessons on the Council of Nicaea and the Council of Trent in a general way, by asking what councils have been mentioned before, what was done there, etc.

The following may need special explanation: "Matters of faith and morals." All that we must believe (faith) and do (morals) in order to be saved.

*Infallible:* cannot make a mistake.

*The faithful:* those who belong to the Church.

Read the lesson over very carefully yourself and make sure that every statement you make is clear and correct.

### Read Lesson 34

Go over the lesson again, paragraph by paragraph.

The Vatican Council was the 20th and last General or Ecumenical Council held.

In the first paragraph call up in imagination the glorious assembly of bishops and priests, headed by the pope. Picture them listening intently to every word of the Holy Father.

The second paragraph states the truth of the infallibility of the pope. He can make a mistake, of course, in anything that concerns other matters. It is only when he speaks as Chief Shepherd and in matters concerning faith and morals that he is infallible. Show by example just what that means.

The *Te Deum* is a great hymn of praise to God. The "Holy God, We Praise Thy Name" expresses somewhat the same sentiments.

Naturally, since Protestants did not want to obey the pope,

they began to deny that he had a right to tell them what to believe.

Make good use of the Scripture texts as suggested at the end of the lesson. The truths stated in this lesson are attacked especially in our own day. It is well for the children to have the significant texts at their fingers' ends.

Have pupils use Scripture texts to prove their answers in all but the last three numbers.

8. A religious dogma is a truth, such as the Trinity, which the Church teaches, on its infallible authority.

9. The Catholic Church is to be found in all countries.

10. The great missionaries and apostles of the nations, such as St. Patrick, St. Boniface, St. Francis Xavier, etc.

*Teacher's References:*

*Church History,* "Spiritual Triumphs," pages 540–542.

*Catholic Action Series,* Book I, Chap. III, "The Unity of the Church."

*Teacher's Notes:*

### Lesson 35

*Aim:* To learn how the Blessed Mother herself seemed to approve of the decision of the Church, by appearing at Lourdes and referring to herself as the Immaculate Conception.

*Preparation:* Show pictures of Our Lady of Lourdes and of the saints that are special patrons of purity.

Since the Feast of St. Bernadette of Lourdes is celebrated just at this time, concentrate your activities around the feast itself. In that case all the little booklets the children have made could be exhibited and a special little program held on that day.

Review the religious teachings explained by the Vatican Council and especially the pope's earlier announcement of Mary's Immaculate Conception. We have already heard that Mary herself must have been pleased with her title, "Immaculate Conception." We shall now hear the story of her appearance at Lourdes, where she said of herself: "I am the Immaculate Conception."
*Read Lesson 35*

After the first reading and discussion, arrange the story into little scenes for different members of the class to dramatize. Also give one or the other little play mentioned in the references or taken from some other source. Be sure to read the story again in its entirety after the children have enjoyed the dramatizations, keeping in mind the teaching of the Church which is exemplified in this lesson; namely, that Mary was conceived without stain of original sin.

Impress very deeply upon the children the points suggesting how to keep pure.

*Practical Application*

Use the lily, emblem of purity, as a motif for designs on posters, blackboard, booklets, etc.

It is well in this day and age to make much of the virtue of purity. Plan to devote the entire week especially to thoughts and activities centering around the beauty of holy purity as exemplified in Mary Immaculate. Make the work as attractive as possible. Be careful not to make the children feel that because they have failed in this regard, they are hopelessly debased. Aim at lifting up rather than casting down.

Let there be a certain joy in all your suggestions and activities.

Take this opportunity also to direct the children's thoughts to higher and holier things. Call attention to the fact that we may acquire habits of thought that are not good and make definite suggestions for breaking any such habits that children may have acquired.

Guard against making the children believe that there is sin where there is none.

*Things to Do:*

1. Let the children tell some few details about these saints.

2. "My Queen! My Mother! Remember I am thine own. Keep me, as thy property and possession." (Indulgence of 40 days each time. Pius IX, Aug. 5, 1851.)

4. See reference to *Catholic School Journal* at the end of the lesson.

5. Refer the children also to magazines used in the homes.

6. A simpler booklet might be made by just folding a sheet of paper, pasting a picture of the Blessed Virgin on the outside and writing a prayer or poem on the inside.

7. March 25. This would be a good opportunity to review the Hail Mary and to learn more about its significance.

8, 9. Here is a chance to let the pupils exercise a choice. It is important in matters immaterial to give pupils such opportunities frequently in order that they might learn to make decisions for themselves and do a little thinking of their own.

Do not let the quotations go unexplained.

*Can You Answer These Questions?*

1. No. Some people deceive others or are themselves deceived. Others have too lively an imagination.

2. The Church; that is, the confessor, the bishop, etc.

3. We use holy water to ask God's blessing and protection from the powers of darkness.

4. We should use holy water at night before going to sleep, on entering the church, in time of temptations, etc.

5. No. Sacramentals do not always keep us from harm. Their power depends entirely upon the will of God. They do not act as a charm.

6. Original sin.

7. From actual sin.

8. Original sin is the name of the sin we inherit from our first parents, while actual sin is sin that we commit ourselves.

9. The Sixth Commandment.

10. The Sixth Commandment forbids all immodesty with ourselves or others in looks, dress, words, or actions.

*Return to Introduction to This Unit:*

As a final summary or clinching or organization of this unit, return to its introductory statement and read it again and discuss in the light of all the material of the unit.

*Teacher's References:*

*Catholic Action Series,* Book II, Chap. XXII, "Holy Purity."

"The Miracle Lady of Lourdes," *C.S.J.,* February, 1934.

"Sight to the Blind," *C.S.J.,* February, 1935.

*Teacher's Notes:*

*Scripture Texts:*

This exercise is intended as a little test in the use of finding Scripture texts and also in applying the text to some important truth learned.

If there is no way of having each child work out the entire test, let individual children look for just one text each and write it out and then have all the children participate in applying the text to some important teaching of the Church.

1. "Going, therefore, teach ye all nations, baptizing them in the name of the Father, and of the Son, and of the Holy Ghost."

2. "He that heareth you heareth Me; and he that despiseth you, despiseth Me. And he that despiseth Me, despiseth Him that sent Me."

3. "I am the Vine; you are the branches: he that abideth in Me, and I in him, the same beareth much fruit: for without Me you can do nothing."

4. "Thomas answered and said to Him: My Lord, and my God."

5. "And behold a voice from heaven saying: This is My beloved Son in whom I am well pleased."

6. "Jesus saith to him: I am the way and the truth, and the life. No man cometh to the Father but by Me."

7. "And suddenly there came a sound from heaven, as of a mighty wind coming, and it filled the whole house where they were sitting. And there appeared to them parted tongues as it were of fire, and sat upon every one of them: And they were filled with the Holy Ghost, and they began to speak with divers tongues, according as the Holy Ghost gave them to speak."

8. "And I say to thee: That thou art Peter; and upon this rock I will build My church, and the gates of hell shall not prevail against it."

9. Substitute for this, John x. 16. "And other sheep I have that are not of this fold; them also I must bring, and they shall hear My voice, and there shall be one fold and one shepherd."

10. "And Jesus said: Father, forgive them, for they know not what they do. But they, dividing His garments, cast lots."

11. "Blessed are the clean of heart: for they shall see God."

12. "And whilst they were eating, Jesus took bread; and blessing, broke, and gave to them and said: Take ye, This is My body. And having taken the chalice, giving thanks He gave it to them. And they all drank of it. And He said to them: This is My blood of the new testament, which shall be shed for many."

13. "Jesus saith to him: If thou wilt be perfect, go sell what thou hast, and give to the poor, and thou shalt have treasure in heaven; and come, follow Me."

14. "He said, therefore, to them again: Peace be to you. As the Father hath sent Me, I also send you."

15. "For what doth it profit a man if he gain the whole world, and suffer the loss of his own soul? Or what exchange shall a man give for his soul?"

# UNIT XI

# THE CHURCH, MOTHER OF ALL PEOPLE

*Time:* Second half of April.

## Feasts to Remember

April 23 St. George
(Patron of England.)

25 St. Mark, Evangelist
(Have the pupils read a simple story directly from the Gospel of St. Mark, such as that found in x. 13–16.)

## *The Unit Introduction:*

In the course of this reading have the pupils recall from past lessons what the Church has done to show herself a true mother to her children. Call for specific examples by asking questions such as the following:

How did the Church teach her children to love one another?

What was the work of the deacons in the early Christian times (Lesson 4)?

Who taught the barbarian nations to live peacefully with one another?

Who taught them to cultivate the soil?

Explain what is meant by "the oppressed." If a person is treated unjustly, if he has to work harder than he is able, if, in a word, he is treated as a slave, we say that he is oppressed.

Read the introduction again at the close of the unit, in order to tie up the two lessons more closely.

## Lesson 36

*Aim:* To understand more clearly the words "Thou shalt love thy neighbor as thyself," especially as they are carried out by the Church as the Mother of all people.

*Preparation:* Because the Church's teaching in regard to social justice is so little recognized today, be well prepared to present it in as clear and effective a manner as possible.

Read the references referring to social justice.

It would be well to have the children read some of the suggested stories ahead of time. "The Nuremberg Stove" will give them a good idea of the care and love lavished upon a single piece of work.

We are all branches of the same Vine. Therefore we should help one another and contribute to one another's welfare and happiness. We shall learn in this lesson how the Church helps us to carry out Christ's teachings to love one another.

### Read Lesson 36

Each paragraph will need careful explanation:

1. In paragraph one try to give a good picture of family life at the time when each man did his work at home. Perhaps the men who carved some of the beautiful woodwork for the great Gothic cathedrals did the carving in their homes. Imagine the whole family interested, watching every new development. The boys are eager to help along, the father explains the symbolism. The piece of furniture or statuary almost becomes part of their lives. They are not eager to get it finished. They are interested in making it as perfect as possible, for it belongs to the house of God. "A thing of beauty is a joy forever."

2. Then came machinery which had to be put into large buildings. The father and the boys had to leave home to work. They were poorly paid, because those who owned the machines thought only of themselves. Sometimes the mother had to go too, and even young children. The home was neglected, the machinery was often unsafe, factories unhealthful.

3. The Church, the good Mother, was the only one who spoke for the poor. Men and women devoted their lives to the relief of the unfortunate poor and suffering.

4. Make sure that the word *encyclical* is well understood and impress upon the children the importance of such letters and

that our attitude toward them should be that of reverence and simple obedience.

Explain especially the four points set forth by the bishops, but remember to simplify the thoughts as much as possible.

*a*) In the first point we come back to the thought that man is made for heaven. If he loves gold so much that it makes him forget God entirely, he cannot save his soul.

*b*) This point brings out the dignity of man. Man has not only a body but also a soul. Being made according to the image of God, he must be treated with a certain respect. He must not be treated as a slave with no rights.

*c*) Recall here the Vine and the Branches. We all belong together to the same Vine. We must love one another. That holds true of the workingman and employer as well as of other people.

*d*) This applies to a system of labor which tends to destroy family life. Not much can be said here to young children. It may be pointed out to them that God wants people to live together in families. The father should support the family, the mother should keep house and look after the children and all should live together and try to make the home as happy as possible. When father and mother both have to go to work, they cannot care for and train their children as they ought.

Be sure to make the children understand that wealth is not harmful in itself but only when it means more to us than God and our souls.

*Ask Yourself:*

The problems are intended to make children aware of faults which are too often overlooked. Pupils should discuss them thoroughly so that they realize their obligations to others. Again, it is not in each case a question of sin. It is, however, a question of training in habits of honesty and fairness. A few suggestions are here added.

1. Whether it is only a game or not, Benny is cheating just the same, and cheating is wrong. Besides, he is forming the habit of dishonesty and giving bad example to his little brother.

2. She is unfair in all three cases. To the teacher, who will not find out that Mayme needs help; to the class, because she may be rated higher than some of the others who do their own work honestly; and to herself, because she goes to school to learn and instead she is only pretending that she knows her lesson.

3. The money does not belong to Ted, therefore he may not keep it. He must give it to the storekeeper who should decide what is to be done with it.

4. Don is unjust to his little brother Pat. He should keep his promise. He is forming a very bad habit. It is such little acts as this that gradually lead to greater dishonesty and injustice.

5. Edna is not just. Since both did an equal share of work, they should share the pay equally.

6. Fred is dishonest, for he pretends that the groceries cost more than they actually do. Furthermore, he is unjust to the grocer, for the mother may blame him for overcharging and buy her groceries somewhere else in the future.

7. Viola is unjust to the maid who gets the blame; to her mother against whom the maid may bear a grudge for blaming her. At the same time she herself is forming a habit of dishonesty by keeping silent when she should have admitted her guilt.

8. Lorraine is unfair to the group. They have as much right as she to take the lead. She must not think herself better than the rest and she must learn to be thoughtful of other people's rights.

9. Carol is guilty of lying in the first place and also of deceit, because she pretends that the lady is not grateful. She is also being unjust to the old lady who will be looked upon as ungrateful by her mother. Even if the old lady did not say "Thank you," Carol is depriving her of food and herself a chance for an act of charity.

(The teacher must be careful not to make these faults, usually thoughtless on the part of the children, seem too serious. The examples are intended to instill right principles in the children.)

10. Dolly wrongs the teacher by lying about her, her mother by causing her to do something she should not do, and herself by losing the chance of a Catholic education.

11. Leo wrongs his father who gets into a quarrel with the neighbor, his neighbor by lying about him and causing him to get into a quarrel, and himself by telling a lie.

12. Len and his brother are being unfair to the other children who get no milk and are also learning to be deceitful.

13. Henry has cheated. He has no right to the money. He is not fair to himself, for he is developing a habit of dishonesty.

14. Kenneth is cheating the customer, being unfair to his father who may lose some of these customers, and taking money which does not belong to him and which he is obliged to restore.

*Things to Do:*

1. Be sure that whatever is planned is well within the means of the child and not too difficult to undertake. Individual children might give an apple to a poor child, etc.

2. It may be well to show here how one machine has taken the place of many men. There is no question here of condemning modern inventions, of course.

3. These questions intend to bring out the fact that this stove was something of an individual thing, one of those masterpieces which the lesson speaks about. Most of the things we use now are turned out by the hundreds, the same in size, shape, quality, and design. Therefore they are not valuable from an artistic point of view.

4. Be sure to apply the text to the lesson.

5. There is a dramatization in the *Catholic School Journal*, March, 1931.

6. The *Medal Stories* fit in well.

7. Have the children tell who spoke the words and on what occasion.

8. Let the children tell of something they have made all by themselves. Also, offer them opportunity in school to do a piece

of work alone. It may not look so well, but it offers immense satisfaction and inspires confidence. It is understood that a child's efforts, no matter how crude, should receive commendation.

## Can You Answer These Questions?

1. Thou shalt love the Lord thy God with thy whole heart, and with thy whole soul, and with thy whole strength.

2. The Seventh Commandment forbids us to steal.

3. The Tenth Commandment forbids us to wish for our neighbor's goods.

4. By envy we mean being sorry over our neighbor's good fortune and success.

5. This depends upon the nature of the act. It may be in the form of injuring one's character and is then against the Eighth Commandment — injuring property, against the Seventh Commandment, injuring the body, against the Fifth, etc.

6. They who have taken goods unlawfully must make restitution.

7. Yes, people should try to make money in order to keep themselves in health and comfort, and so that they will not become a burden to others.

8. Not all rich people are unjust and hard-hearted. But there is great danger that they may become so.

9. The First Commandment teaches us that we must adore but one God.

10. The First Commandment forbids all sins against faith, hope, and charity; also idolatry, superstition, and sacrilege.

## Teacher's References:

*Catholic Action Series,* Book III, Chapters VIII and IX.

*Church History,* "The Pontificate of Leo XIII," pages 578–580; "Leo XIII," pages 283–287.

## Teacher's Notes:

## Lesson 37

*Aim:* To learn from the life of St. Vincent de Paul the great works of charity the Church has undertaken through her saints, especially for the poor and needy.

*Preparation:* Be prepared to give some information about the work of the society of St. Vincent de Paul for the poor. The founder, Frederick Ozanam, will be treated in another lesson. Stress here the work of the Church for the poor.

Have pictures of the Sisters of St. Vincent de Paul and of others that represent works of charity. The little books known as the *Medal Stories* offer splendid material.

Have a picture of a galley ship.

Approach the lesson by asking the children how poor people are cared for by the State and the Church today. Point out that the Church has always had a special care of the poor. A great many saints devoted their entire lives to the poor and unfortunate. Today we shall hear about a saint who is the special patron of charity.

### Read Lesson 37

If possible, read also the life of St. Charles Borromeo or some other saint devoted especially to the poor.

Discuss from paragraph to paragraph, the character traits of St. Vincent, particularly his love for the poor.

### Things to Do:

1. Point out that this love of God naturally overflows to our neighbor.

2. Have the children give other details of St. Vincent's life that may be found elsewhere.

3. Refer to the film "Ben Hur," which the children may have seen.

4. Remember to connect the drawing closely with the lesson by calling for a repetition of the story itself.

5. The *Medal Stories* will be of help here.

6. This may be done for oral language work.

7. See also *Catholic Action Series*, Book II, page 326.

8. Let this be a voluntary act, done without direction.

9. Perhaps you can have someone else come to the classroom to talk about this work of the parish.

### Can You Answer These Questions?

1. Thou shalt love the Lord thy God.

2. Everybody is our neighbor.

3. We must love all people and not only those who do good to us.

4. That is a form of lying and cheating and is wrong.

5. Because we are all members of the Mystical Body of Christ and should help one another for His sake.

### Return to Introduction to This Unit:

As a final summary or clinching or organization of this unit, return to its introductory statement and read it again and discuss in the light of all the material of the unit.

*Teacher's References:*

*Church History,* "St. Vincent de Paul, Apostle of Organized Charity," pages 497–500.

*Catholic Action Series,* Book III, Chap. VI.

*Test Yourself:*

Answers:

1. Cross
2. Three
3. Holy Ghost
4. One, holy, Catholic, Apostolic
5. Church
6. Pope
7. Nations
8. Apostles
9. Jesus — God
10. Infallible
11. Forever
12. Holy Orders
13. Dead, Grave
14. Heaven
15. Hell
16. Commandments
17. Neighbor

*Teacher's Notes:*

# UNIT XII

## THE CHURCH, MOTHER OF SAINTS

*Time:* First half of May.

### Feasts to Remember

May  *1  SS. Philip and James, Apostles
          (Have the pupils find where they labored for the
          spread of the Church and how they died.)

      *3  Finding of the Cross
          (Lesson 14.)

      *4  St. Monica
          (Have the pupils review the story of St. Augustine,
          Lesson 8.)

     *14  St. Boniface
          (Review Lesson 31.)

     *15  St. John Baptist de la Salle
          (Lesson 26.)

### *The Unit Introduction:*

See how many saints the pupils can enumerate for each
group mentioned. Let them go over the lessons learned so far
and list the saints under their various occupations, adding others
that they know to the list.

Point out that sanctity does not consist in doing extraordinary
things, but in doing the ordinary things of life in an extraordinary way. View the saints not only as individuals who have
lived holy lives, but also as instruments in the hands of God to
further the work of His Church. For that reason the question
should frequently be asked: "What was this particular saint's
work for the Church?"

## Lesson 38

*Aim:* To learn how Francis de Sales became a great saint of the Church by practicing especially the little virtues.

*Preparation:* Have the Eight Beatitudes ready to read. Appoint little groups for dramatizations.

We sometimes think that to be a saint we have to do great things. We shall learn from our story of today of one saint who became great just by doing the little things well.

*Read Lesson 38*

Explain such expressions as "brilliant career," "to win back to the faith," etc. Pick out paragraph by paragraph, the little virtues practiced by St. Francis.

*Practical Application*

Make clear the meaning of each of the virtues mentioned, by specific examples.

Dwell particularly on those that have not been stressed in the past, such as thoughtfulness and cheerfulness. Thoughtfulness shows that we are thinking of others and trying to see what we can do for them, even before they ask.

Simple posters bearing mottoes such as "Be kind," "Smile," etc., with suitable pictures, will prove effective for this lesson.

Help the children to cultivate a cheerful, sunny disposition. A bright "good morning" as they enter the classroom and a cheerful response on the part of the teacher, will do much to form the habit of cheerfulness.

In the sayings of St. Francis, let the children do their own choosing.

*Things to Do:*

1. The feast is August 21.

2. At times remind individual pupils who are hasty, of the use of this prayer.

3. Padua is in Italy. What great saint lived in Padua?

4. Stories referred to in the text ought to be read for review. They may be assigned for silent reading.

5. Be sure to talk over these little virtues somewhat at length.

6. The Beatitudes could be memorized. (See Teacher's References.)

7. The Good Shepherd, Jesus Blessing the Children, Jesus and Mary Magdalen.

8. Gentleness — anger, rudeness; kindness — unkindness; thoughtfulness — thoughtlessness; cheerfulness — ill temper; Christian politeness — impoliteness.

9. These pictures, if properly selected, should prove a great help in impressing the little virtues on the pupils.

10. Let the children find them in their readers, magazines, etc. *The School Mate* will be of special help.

11, 12. Use another period for this work if necessary.

*Can You Answer These Questions?*

1. Anger is against the Fifth Commandment.

2. Gentleness is the opposite virtue.

3. Lying is against the Eighth Commandment.

4. Truthfulness is the opposite virtue.

5. Sins against the Eighth Commandment are: rash judgments, backbiting, slanders, and lies (these sins should be explained).

Review particularly the Eighth Commandment.

*Teacher's References:*

*Bible Stories for Children,* Sister Anna Louise, "The Sermon on the Mount." (This lesson gives a good interpretation for children.)

*Catholic Action Series,* Book III, "The Daily Check," pages 35–36.

*Teacher's Notes:*

## Lesson 39

*Aim:* To learn from the saints in all stations of life, how we, too, as branches of the true Vine, can and should become saints.

*Preparation:* Find pictures of different women saints. Talk about the women who have been mentioned so far in the text, and their share in the work of the Church. Women have always taken part in the Church's work side by side with the men. We shall hear about more of them today.

### Read Lesson 39

If possible, have the children find out more about the saints mentioned and add bits of information as the lesson is discussed paragraph by paragraph. A different saint might be assigned to each member of the class and the information called for as the lesson is reviewed.

*Practical Application*

Teach or review a hymn in honor of a favorite or patron saint. Explain that today, too, there are women needed in the mission fields to help the missionary priests.

Be sure that the little practices the children choose are not too difficult. While it is desirable to remind them from time to time of the resolution, constantly aim at making them self-reliant, for you are training them for life and not for school.

**Things to Do:**

1. It must have taken a holy mother to train a child in holiness.

3. St. Lucy is patron against diseases of the eyes.

4. Feast on February 6.

6. Let the children do as much as possible themselves. It is part of their training in self-reliance.

7. Make your explanation short and simple.

8. See what they choose for themselves. Give as little help as possible. Remember, it is not so much to be an elaborate program as a purposeful activity teaching pupils appreciation of their religious teachers.

9. In the beginning of the fourteenth century France had so strong a hold on the affairs of the church that the residence of the popes was moved from Rome to Avignon, a city on the borderland of France. For nearly seventy years the popes, all Frenchmen, lived in this city under the influence of the French kings. This period of time is known in Church History as the "Babylonian Captivity" because it lasted about as long as the captivity of the Jews in Babylon. All Christianity felt grieved over this state of affairs. It was Catherine of Siena who, in 1376, went in person to Avignon and begged Gregory XI to come back to Rome. He did so on the 17th of January, 1377.

10. Such pictures can easily be found in missionary magazines.

11. Review the lesson on Cathedral Builders.

12. Perhaps the children can find other short sayings.

13. Carving, making roses, cutting out a banner, etc., are other activities.

14. See the *St. Gregory Hymnal.*

Let the children find when the feasts occur for the saints mentioned.

*Can You Answer These Questions?*

1. On November 1.

2. The Sacraments through which we obtain grace.

3. Grace is a supernatural gift of God given to us through the merits of Jesus Christ to help us save our souls.

4. There are two kinds of grace, sanctifying grace and actual grace.

5. Faith, hope, and love.

6. Review the acts they have already learned.

7. Actual grace is that help which enlightens our mind and makes us want to keep away from evil and do good.

8. Yes, without grace we can do nothing to gain heaven.

9. The saints had free will just as we have, therefore they could have refused the grace of God.

*Teacher's References:*

*Journal of Religious Instruction,* "Consider the Lives of the Saints," November, 1934.

*Church History,* "The Babylonian Captivity of the Popes," pages 396–403.

*Catholic School Journal,* "Origin of All Saints' Day" (play), November, 1933.

*Teacher's Notes:*

## Lesson 40

*Aim:* To learn what the Church has done through her missionaries and saints to spread the Faith in the North American missions.

*Preparation:* Explain: ignorant; superstitious; lay brother; layman.

Introduce the lesson by recalling the missionaries that followed in the footsteps of Columbus. In the beginning they labored principally in South America, Central America, and Mexico. Somewhat later, missionaries came also to North America. We shall hear today about the Jesuit Martyrs of North America who suffered untold cruelties and gave their lives to save the souls of the Indians. How precious must have been a single soul in the eyes of these great missionaries.

*Read Lesson 40*

The opening scene of this lesson is especially suitable for dramatization.

Since the lesson finds us on home ground, utilize the opportunity to bring in the work of the Church in correlation with American History. We find religious names for cities, rivers, lakes, etc. These names are an indication of the spirit of faith with which the early missionaries and explorers were imbued. List some of these names:

San Francisco, San Antonio, St. Croix, Santa Fe, St. Lawrence River, Maryland.

*Practical Application*

Plan as far as possible to correlate American History with this lesson.

Have one of the children write for the *Indian Sentinel* if you do not get it.

Neat little scrapbooks, especially with sacred pictures from such magazines as the *Sacred Heart Messenger,* can be easily made, and make an acceptable gift for Indian children.

*Things to Do:*

1. Point out also Auriesville, N. Y., the home of Katherine Tekakwitha.

2. Aim to make the children feel a personal interest and concern for the Indian Missions. Catholic Indians, too, are branches of the true Vine, members of the Mystical Body of Christ.

3. See children's list in text.

4. Perhaps the poem in the reading list could be used as a dramatization.

5. Correlate your history work as much as possible with such lessons as this.

6–11. Correlate with your history lesson, if possible.

12. This gives opportunity for a bit of local history which should help to bring the lesson closer home. Make much of the information you may get. Possibly a trip to some interesting local site can be added.

13. This should be prepared ahead of time by some pupil.

14. See reading list in text.

*Can You Answer These Questions?*

1. Father Jogues' consecrated fingers were missing.

2. Father Jogues had shed his blood for love of Christ. It was only right that he should be permitted to say Mass and there drink of the Blood of Christ.

3. To be superstitious means to believe that creatures have a power which God alone has.

4. It is against the first commandment.

5. Sins against faith, hope, and charity (explain in detail, if necessary).

6. It is not superstitious to wear a blessed medal.

7. Wearing a four-leaved clover, using a horseshoe for good luck, etc.

*Return to Introduction to This Unit:*

As a final summary or clinching or organization of this unit, return to its introductory statement and read it again and discuss in the light of all the material of the unit.

*Teacher's References:*

*Church History,* "The Jesuit Martyrs of America."

*Catholic Action Series,* Book I, "Modern Missionaries," pages 49–51.

*Test Yourself:*

(Answers)

8. Encyclical

1. Ireland

10. Clovis

9. Sisters of Charity

5. Lima

4. China

2. Tree of Thor

3. Holland

6. Vatican

7. Immaculate Conception

*Teacher's Notes:*

*Teacher's Notes:*

# UNIT XIII

## OTHER LEADERS OF THE CHURCH

*Time:* Second half of May.

### Feasts to Remember

May *25   St. Gregory VII
            (Lesson 17.)
   *     Pentecost
           Holy Trinity
           (Recall St. Patrick and the shamrock; also, St. Augustine at the seashore.)
   *     Corpus Christi
           (Review Lesson 22 in connection with this feast and sing some of the beautiful hymns which St. Thomas wrote.)
 *30   St. Angela Merici
           (Lesson 39.)

### *The Unit Introduction:*

Impress upon the pupils their own obligations to respond to the Holy Father's call to Catholic Action. Have them tell how they can take a part in Catholic Action. When you come back at the end of the unit to read the introduction again, call to the pupils' minds especially the deep love these great leaders bore for their faith, and aim to arouse a similar love and devotion in their own hearts.

In the review let the children tell what, in particular, each of these men did for the Church.

### Lesson 41

*Aim:* To gain through the study of the life of St. Thomas More a fuller knowledge and appreciation of that unconquerable faith which shone so brilliantly in this great champion of the Church's rights.

*Preparation:* Explain the following: bribe; resigned; oath; supreme.

Ask questions such as the following: Who started the Great Revolution? In what country did it start? Was Germany the only country that was torn away from the Church? Today we shall read of one of the great champions of the Faith in England at the time of the Great Revolution.

*Read Lesson 41*

Thomas More was a great scholar; that is, he studied and read much and also wrote a number of books, one of which, *Utopia,* is still widely read.

The words of Sir Thomas in the third last paragraph will need explanation. Recall that Saul, who later became St. Paul, was present at the stoning of Stephen and consented to it. Sir Thomas says that as Paul and Stephen are now friends in heaven so also he hopes that he and the king will both be friends in heaven. Since this lesson was written, Thomas More was canonized and is now St. Thomas More. Have the pupils note the date of his canonization in their textbooks. It is May 19, 1935. Bishop Fisher was canonized at the same time. If there is time, relate something of the bishop's life in connection with this lesson.

*Things to Do:*

1. The chapel scene would lend itself well to the week's work on the Mass.

2. Beautifully colored metallic paper makes up most attractively.

3. The pictures can be obtained from church goods catalogs. Rubber stamps are offered for the purpose and add much interest to such an activity as this. (See General References.)

4. Change this topic, if necessary, to suit your own needs.

5. The sacrifice of Isaac and that of Melchisedech are appropriate.

6. Show the class exactly what to do at the time of elevation. Have them raise their heads to look up at the Sacred Host and

say the words of St. Thomas, the Apostle, and then bow their heads in adoration. (Remind them of the Indulgence, of seven years and seven quarantines given by Pope Pius X, May 8, 1907, for this.) The same should be repeated at the elevation of the chalice.

7, 8. Associate the story with the Mass.

*Can You Answer These Questions?*

1. As often as possible; every day if there is an opportunity.

2. Praying the Mass with the priest.

3. Offertory, Elevation, Holy Communion.

4. (See the Missal.)

5. The first Mass was said at the Last Supper.

6. "Do this in commemoration of Me."

7. On all Sundays and holydays of obligation.

8, 9. December 8, Immaculate Conception — Mary's being conceived without sin.

December 25, Christmas — Birth of Christ.

January 1, Circumcision.

Forty Days after Easter, Ascension.

August 15, Assumption of the Blessed Virgin Mary — the Blessed Virgin Mary entering into heaven bodily.

November 1, All Saints — all the saints of God in one celebration.

*Teacher's References:*

Montessori, *The Mass Explained to Children.*

*Catholic Action Series,* Book III, pages 3–14.

*Church History,* "Henry VIII Repudiates the Papacy," pages 446–450.

*Journal of Religious Instruction,* "Helping the Child to be a Part of the Mass," February, 1931.

*Catholic School Journal,* "Teaching the Mass to Children," September, 1934; "Learning to Pray the Mass," November, 1933; "Learning the Mass," February, 1935.

*Teacher's Notes:*

## Lesson 42

*Aim:* To learn of the splendid work of Daniel O'Connell in behalf of the oppressed Catholics of Ireland.

*Preparation:* Approach the story by a review of Lesson 30 which shows how Ireland became a Christian country through the apostolic work of St. Patrick and his monks.

*Read Lesson 42*

Explain what is meant by being a representative in the English Parliament. The Irish were ruled by the English and had no rights of their own. They felt that at least one Irishman ought to speak for them when the English met to make laws, etc. They wanted Daniel O'Connell to be their representative.

What other men have you read about that refused to sign or take an oath? (St. Louis, Thomas More.)

"Four million Irishmen were willing to stand by him." This shows how Daniel O'Connell had united all the Irish Catholics into a strong party.

*Practical Application*

Explain simply how habits are formed by constant repetition of an act, and how hard it is to break them afterwards. It is, therefore, most important that we form as many good habits as possible and avoid bad habits.

Some of the quotations will require explanation, all of them should be talked over. The quotations might appear in large letters on the bulletin or blackboard for discussion during the week.

*Can You Answer These Questions?*

1. An oath is the calling upon God to witness the truth of what we say.

2. We may take an oath when it is ordered by lawful authority or required for God's honor or for our own or our neighbor's good.

3. The Eighth Commandment forbids us to lie.

4. The Eighth Commandment also forbids us to judge rashly, to backbite, and to slander others.

*Teacher's References:*

*Church History,* "Catholic Emancipation in the British Isles," pages 529–531.

*Catholic Action Series,* Book II, "How to Acquire a Habit," pages 409–411.

*Teacher's Notes:*

## Lesson 43

*Aim:* To learn of the work of Frederick Ozanam in spreading the Christian faith and Christian charity in France at a time when the Church was losing many of its members in that country.

*Preparation:* Approach the lesson by recalling the work of St. Vincent de Paul among the poor. More than two hundred years later, in the same city, a society was started, which bore the name of St. Vincent de Paul. The young man who founded this society, which is doing so much good today, was Frederick Ozanam, about whom the lesson treats.

A picture of St. Vincent de Paul and of the Sisters of Charity should be on the bulletin board.

### Read Lesson 43

Frederick Ozanam loved his faith. Note how he prayed in the time of temptation to remain true to the Church. In your discussion of the story, show that the temptation itself is not a sin. We, too, are often tempted in different ways. Like Frederick Ozanam, we must pray to God to keep us from falling into sin.

Here we have a layman devoting himself heart and soul to the spread of the faith. What a splendid example of Catholic Action!

### Practical Application

Make much of the practice of counting the blessings God sends us. How much better it is to be happy and grateful for the many things we have, than to find fault and grumble about the things we have not. Encourage the children to carry this practice with them through life. Call attention frequently to God's gifts, to prayers answered and favors received, and stop then and there to make an act of thanksgiving aloud. Impress upon the pupils the thought that they must always be grateful to God for favors received.

### Things to Do:

1. This will help make children aware of their many blessings. Include in the list the gift of faith, citizenship in a civilized country, the privilege of attending a Catholic school.

2. Let the children get the information and tell the class about it.

3. Make the practice simple and in keeping with the circumstances.

4. Michelangelo, Timothy.

5. If the pupils have a missal, call their attention to the special collects for the Mass of Thanksgiving.

*Can You Answer These Questions?*

1. The Church teaches us what we must believe to be saved.

2. Temptation is no sin if we do not desire it or give way to it.

3. Pray, do something else.

4. Faith.

5. A person sins against faith (1) by not trying to know what God has taught; (2) by refusing to believe what God has taught; and (3) by neglecting to profess his belief in what God has taught.

6. We may not deny our faith.

7. We fail to try to know what God has taught by neglecting to learn all we can about our religion.

8. They who do not believe all that God has taught are called heretics and infidels.

*Return to Introduction to This Unit:*

As a final summary or clinching or organization of this unit, return to its introductory statement and read it again and discuss in the light of all the material of the unit.

*Teacher's References:*

*Catholic Encyclopedia,* "Frederick Ozanam."

*Catholic Action Series,* Book III, "The Society of St. Vincent de Paul," pages 473–475.

*Catholic School Journal,* "God's Gift of Trees" (design), September, 1934.

*Test Yourself:*

(Answers)

1. Daniel O'Connell
2. St. Stephen
3. St. Augustine
4. Frederick Ozanam
5. Queen Blanche
6. St. Paul
7. Michelangelo
8. St. Thomas Aquinas
9. St. Francis de Sales
10. St. Teresa

*Teacher's Notes:*

# UNITS XIV AND XV

## THE CHURCH AND PEACE
## YOU ARE THE BRANCHES

*Time:* June.

### Feasts to Remember

June *5 St. Boniface
(Lesson 31.)

11 St. Barnabas, Apostle
Call attention also at this time to the important feasts of the summer vacation, especially the feast of the Assumption on August 15.

### *The Unit Introduction:*

Read the introduction to Unit XIV carefully with the pupils and review it as usual after the lesson itself has been read.

Before reading the introduction to Unit XV read Lesson I in order to relate it more intimately with the final unit, which completes the thought. Be sure to point out the relationship between the two lessons.

If the pupils are equal to it, let them read St. John, Chapter XV, directly from the Bible. They will recognize many of the verses. To make the reading more impressive, let the class imagine that they are the disciples of our Lord and that they are grouped around Him while He is speaking these serious and beautiful words directly to them. In that case read the words for them, slowly and devoutly.

### Lesson 44

*Aim:* In this lesson aim to show what the Church has done to bring about peace and give the pupils at least some elementary knowledge of the present-day attempts at world peace and the main reason for failure — refusal to observe the law of charity according to the teachings of Christ.

*Preparation:* As this lesson is rather difficult for young children, it will be necessary to prepare it very carefully.

Have on hand, if possible, a good-sized picture of Christ surrounded by children of all nationalities. Talk about the picture and show that the law of God "Thou shalt love thy neighbor as thyself" binds all of us to love all nations and to hate no one.

### Read Lesson 44

Discuss the lesson paragraph by paragraph.

Be sure to explain difficult passages such as "he fearlessly protested against the wrong," "he remained strictly neutral," and particularly make clear the Holy Father's words: "The Gospel does not contain one law of charity for individuals," etc.

### Ask Yourself:

Discuss these thoughts at length, especially such as come closest to the children's experiences.

### Things to Do:

1. See Campion, Book III, page 255.

3. This is the picture of the little boy Christ among the animals which sometimes bears the title "And a little child shall lead them." It is very beautiful and should be shown to the children if possible (Catechetical Guild, St. Paul, 15 cents).

4. 1914 to 1918 — 4 years. The World War began in 1914 and ended in 1918.

5. Blessed are the peacemakers for they shall possess the land.

6. "Lord Jesus Christ, who said to Thine Apostles, Peace I leave you. . . ."

7. Pope Innocent III.   St. Catherine of Siena.

Read the *Gloria* carefully with the pupils. It is one of the Church's great hymns of praise. We owe God praise and adoration. We should, therefore, say the *Gloria* often, especially with the priest at Mass. It is also an appropriate prayer to say after Holy Communion or when we are filled with joy at the thought of some grace or favor we have received from God.

*Can You Answer These Questions?*

1. Jesus showed that He loved all men when He came to earth to save all and gave His life for all.

2. Jesus died for us because He loved us and wanted all of us to be happy with Him in heaven.

3. If a war is in self-defense it is not wrong.

4. Hatred and quarreling are against the Fifth Commandment.

5. Jesus is the Prince of Peace.

6. He is called the Prince of Peace because He came to bring peace to earth.

7. He came on earth Christmas Day more than 1,930 years ago.

8. See text, page 290.

*Teacher's References:*

*Church History,* Benedict XV, "The Pope of the World War," pages 583–587.

*Catholic Action Series,* Book II, "The Prayer for Peace," pages 178–179, "Blessed are the Peacemakers," page 421; Book III, "International Relations," pages 254–265.

*Teacher's Notes:*

## YOU ARE THE BRANCHES

*Aim:* The aim of this unit is to review and draw more closely together the lessons of the entire year.

*Preparation:* Read over the two lessons of this unit and have as many pictures on hand as possible, referring to the lesson. First of all, the pope, St. Peter's, the Vatican, the amphitheater, the catacombs, etc.

Plan to make the trip to Rome as realistic as possible. You might have maps and time tables on hand and plan the route just as regular travelers do. Also have pictures of steamers, etc.

Read the introductory paragraph and compare it with Lesson 1.

*Read Lesson 45*

Review the various incidents referred to in each paragraph. The following questions may be used:

    I. What happened on the first Pentecost Day?

       Who spoke to the people?

       How many were converted the first day?

       Did the Apostles preach to the Jews only?

       Who is called the Apostle of the Gentiles?

       What two Apostles were thought to be gods?

       What Apostle did not die as a martyr?

To which of his disciples did St. Paul write two epistles?

How did St. Peter die?

How did St. Paul die?

II. What Roman emperor had the Christians burned as torches in his garden?

How long did the persecutions last?

Where did the Christians hide during the persecutions?

How did Constantine win his victory?

Who was the mother of Constantine?

What did she do for the Church?

How did people look upon the cross before the victory of Constantine?

How did they look upon it afterwards?

Who brought the Faith to Ireland? To Scotland? to Germany?

What country was famous for its many monasteries and saints?

III, IV. What did the Church do for the barbarians that swept over Europe?

Were there schools for all children at that time?

What did the monks do in the monastery schools?

What did Charlemagne do for the Church?

What did Charlemagne do for learning?

How did the Church help the emperor?

What great cathedrals were raised in the Middle Ages?

Why were they built with so much care?

How did the people of the Middle Ages learn their religion from the cathedrals?

Who was the greatest sculptor of the Middle Ages?

What statues did he carve?

Who painted the greatest Madonna pictures?

What are the names of two of the greatest Madonna pictures he painted?

Where, in Rome, can we see some of these great paintings today?

Who wrote the greatest religious poem that was ever written?

Through whom was it made possible to do these great works of art?

In what land did Christ live and die?

In the hands of what unbelievers was this land most of the time?

How did the Christians try to win the land back?

Why did the Christians want this land for themselves?

What was the cry of the first crusades?

What saintly king led a crusade?

What saint went from country to country to preach a crusade?

Were the crusades successful?

V. Who was the spiritual father of all Christians down to the end of the Middle Ages?

Who started the Great Revolution?

What was the religion of those called that separated themselves from the Church?

Did they remain united themselves?

What Council was like a skillful doctor?

How did the Church fare after this Council?

What did Protestants say about the sacraments?

Has the Church any enemies today?

Will it be possible to crush her?

What did Christ say about His Church?

How long will the Church last?

How should we feel toward our Church?

What prayer contains the truths that we must believe?

Before reading the last lesson do everything you can to make it enjoyable and to get the right atmosphere. You are traveling as a class. What are you going to take along? What would you like to see? Nearly every subject of the day or week can be correlated intimately with the lesson.

Explain that "Roma" is the Italian for Rome.

*Read Lesson 46*
*Things to Do:*

1. Get as much information as possible about the Vatican City and do not forget the Radio Broadcasting Station over which we hear the voice of the Holy Father. Encourage the children to watch for a broadcast from Vatican City.

2. Let the children find pictures themselves and as many different views as possible.

3. An opportunity for dramatization.

4. Some reading or explanation will be needed here.

5. Booklets from steamship companies will help to make this work more interesting.

6. Be sure to have this talk if at all possible.

7. You might have the entire class read the story once more.

8. The foremost figure to the left in the picture, page 298, is a Swiss Guard. Their uniform is very colorful.

9. May be done for oral language work.

10. Fish, palm, lamp, loaves, etc.

*Now Answer These Questions:*

1. 3,000.

2, 3. The Church is a society of all those who are baptized, who believe in the teachings of Jesus Christ, and who are ruled by those who take the place of Christ on earth; that is, the pope, the bishops, and priests.

4. Pope Pius XI — Jesus Christ.

5. In Rome, St. Peter crucified upside down, St. Paul beheaded.

6. They were tortured, burned, beheaded, etc.

7. Constantine, because he won a victory through the sign of the cross.

8. By the migration of nations.

9. St. Patrick, St. Boniface, and others.

10. Under Charlemagne.

11. Through great works of art such as the Gothic cathedrals, great paintings, and great writings.

12. "Thou art Peter . . . and the gates of hell shall not pre-

vail against it" and "Behold, I am with you all days even to the consummation of the world."

13. The members of the great religious Orders of St. Ignatius, St. Dominic, St. Francis, and others.

14. France, Russia, Mexico.

15. Unbelievers, bigots, atheists, etc.

16. By giving up our belief in what the Church teaches.

17. Pray, receive the sacraments regularly, obey the commandments of God and the Church.

18. Be careful not to expose ourselves to danger by bad company, reading, etc.

19. The Apostles' Creed contains the chief truths which the Catholic Church believes and teaches.

20. The Nicene Creed.

### Return to Introduction to This Unit:

As a final summary or clinching or organization of this unit, return to its introductory statement and read it again and discuss in the light of all the material of the unit.

### Teacher's References:

*Church History,* "The Holy Father's Radio Message to the World," page 599; "Vatican Treaty," page 591.

*Catholic Action Series,* Book II, "The Sermon on the Mount," pages 413–426.

### Teacher's Notes:

*A Game with the Saints:*
(Answers)

1. St. Peter
2. St. Patrick
3. St. Christopher
4. St. Therese (Little Flower)
5. St. Agnes

6. St. Aloysius
7. St. John the Evangelist
8. St. George
9. St. Vincent de Paul
10. St. Andrew

*Special Patrons:*

1. SS. Cosmas and Damian
2. St. Luke
3. St. Vincent de Paul
4. St. Peter Claver
5. St. Francis Xavier
6. St. Isidore
7. St. Joseph
8. St. Hubert

9. St. Christopher
10. St. Caecilia
11. St. Stephen
12. St. Camillus de Lellis
13. St. Martha — Anne
14. St. Gregory
15. St. Appolonia

*Patrons:*

1. St. Boniface
2. Bridget, Patrick
3. St. George
4. St. Andrew
5. St. Genevieve

6. St. Mark
7. St. John the Baptist
8. Immaculate Conception
9. St. James
10. St. Francis Xavier

*Feasts:*

1. St. Therese (Little Flower)
2. St. George
3. Conversion of St. Paul
4. St. Francis de Sales
5. Finding of the Cross
6. Three Kings (Epiphany)
7. Immaculate Conception
8. St. Thomas

9. St. Stephen
10. Our Lady of Lourdes
11. St. Anne
12. Birthday of Our Lady
13. St. John the Baptist
14. St. Teresa of Avila
15. Guardian Angels

*Other Tests Suggested:*

Find saints that were kings.
Find saints that were queens.
Find saints that were laborers.
Find saints that were popes.
Let the pupils plan similar tests of their own.

## TEACHER'S REFERENCES

While the teacher is urged to read widely in preparation for her daily work, there are only three or four books mentioned specifically at the end of each lesson, in order to simplify the problem of buying new texts. The references most frequently used are:

Rousselot, S.J., Grandmaison, S.J., Huby, S.J., D'Arcy, S.J.,: *The Life of the Church* (Sheed and Ward). This book describes the spirit of Catholicism as a force in civilization. It shows this spirit in contact with the world and defines its place in history — both the outward history of nations and the inner history of their dominant figures. It should be read in its entirety by every teacher of Church History who is interested in more than the mere enumeration of historical facts.

Laux, *Church History* (Benziger Brothers, 1932). This book is excellent for details with which every teacher should be thoroughly familiar.

Campion, *Catholic Action Series,* in three books (Wm. H. Sadlier, 1932). This is a splendid high-school text correlating religious doctrine with everyday life. The presentation is short and simple and therefore better adapted for the use of the busy teacher than a more lengthy text.

***Further References:***

Brother Eugene, *A Book of Religion for Elementary Schools* (Wm. H. Sadlier, Inc., 1927). A compendium of Bible and Church History.

S. S. N. D., *Character Calendar* (Bruce Publishing Co., 1931). An excellent study of the lives of the saints with a view to building up ideals of character.

*Art Education Through Religion,* Books I to VIII, Gertrude M. McMunigle (Mentzer, Bush & Co., Chicago). This is a set of books in art work for children, showing how closely religion and art can be correlated.

*Correlation of Art and the Mass* (Practical Drawing Co., 1315 So. Michigan Blvd., Chicago).

*The Music Hour,* Catholic Edition, in five books for grades one to nine (Silver, Burdett & Co., Chicago). These graded books contain a variety of songs, religious hymns, and selections of Gregorian chant and correlate splendidly with the work in religion.

*The St. Gregory Hymnal* (The St. Gregory Guild, 1705 Rittenhouse St., Philadelphia, Pa.).

***Books for Children:***

*Gospel Rhymes* (Sheed and Ward, 63–5th Avenue, New York City).

*Six O'clock Saints,* Windham (Sheed and Ward, $1.25).

*Medal Stories,* by the Daughters of Charity (Brown, Morrison Co., Inc., Lynchburg, Va., 1933). These stories are also sold in the five-and-ten-cent stores in ten-cent editions.

*Story of St. Francis of Assisi,* Sister M. Eleanore.

*Little St. Elizabeth,* Von Schmidt-Pauli (Henry Holt & Co., N. Y.).

*Little St. Therese,* Von Schmidt-Pauli (Henry Holt & Co., N. Y.).

*The Child on His Knees,* Marion Dixon Thayer (The Macmillan Co., N. Y.).

*A Child's Garden of Religion Stories,* Matimore (The Macmillan Co., N. Y.).

*Wonder Stories of God's People,* Matimore (The Macmillan Co., N. Y.).

*Heroes of God's Church,* Matimore (The Macmillan Co., N. Y.).

*Pictures:*

The Perry Pictures, Malden, Mass.

New York Sunday School Commission, 416 LaFayette St., New York City.

The University Prints, 10 Boyd St., Newton, Mass.

The Art Extension Society, Westport, Conn.

The Catechetical Guild, St. Paul, Minn.

*Other Helpful Material for Religious Instruction:*

Creative Education Co., Coughlin Bldg., Mankato, Minn.

Large colored charts with explanation of the Mass.

Rubber-stamp outfit of articles used at Mass and pictures of the saints.

Catechetical Guild, St. Paul, Minn.

The Mass, thirty rubber stamps, $5.

Sick Call Outfit, rubber stamps, $1.

Wooden altar, 12 by 26 inches and miniature articles used at Mass (chalice $3\frac{1}{2}$ inches high).

Pictures and other instructional material.

Co-op Parish Activities Service, Effingham, Ill.

Pictures, films, projects, charts, and every variety of instructional material. Catalog on request.

# RESOURCE LIST

We have collected on the following pages a comprehensive list of all the recommended resources found in this manual. Based on their content and/or their frequent use in this series (often across more than one grade level) we have indicated the most essential of these with an asterisk (*), while resources which may be found on the internet are marked with a cross (†).

## Fifth Grade Teacher Resources

*† *The Holy Bible.*

† *The Catholic Encylopedia*, (New York: Robert Appleton Company, 1907-1912).

* *Art Education through Religion*, Mary G. McMunigle (New York: Mentzer, Bush & Company, 1931).

*Bible Stories for Children*, Sister Anna Louise, S.S.J. (New York: Schwartz, Kirwin & Fauss, 1919-1935).

*A Book of Religion for Catholic Elementary Schools: Compendium of Bible and Church History*, Brother Eugene, O.S.F., Litt.D. (New York: William H. Sadlier, 1927).

*The Catholic Action Series, Books 1-3*, Rev. Raymond J. Campion (New York: William H. Sadlier, Inc., 1928).

*Church History*, Rev. John Joseph Laux (New York: Benziger Brothers, 1930).

*Introduction to the Bible*, Rev. John Joseph Laux (New York: Benziger Brothers, 1932).

*The Life of the Church*, Rousselot, Grandmaison, Huby, D'Arcy (London: Sheed & Ward, 1932).

*The Mass Explained to Children*, Maria Montessori (London: Sheed & Ward, 1932).

*St. Thomas Aquinas*, Jacques Maritain (London: Sheed & Ward, 1931).

† *Teacher's Handbook to Bible History*, Rev. A. Urban (New York: Joseph F. Wagner, 1905).

## Fifth Grade Student Readers

*(This list is provided for reference purposes; the majority of recommended readings from these books has been included in a newly published anthology reader to accompany this series.)*

*The American Cardinal Reader, Book Five*, Edith M. McLaughlin (New York: Benziger Brothers, 1930).

*The American Fifth Reader for Catholic Schools*, The School Sisters of Notre Dame (Boston: D.C. Heath and Company, 1930).

*Cathedral Basic Readers, Book Five*, Rev. John A. O'Brien, Ph.D. (Chicago: Scott, Foresman and Company, 1932).

*Catholic Education Series Fifth Reader*, Thomas Edward Shields (Washington, D.C.: The Catholic Education Press, 1915).

*Catholic Education Series Religion Fourth Book*, Thomas Edward Shields (Washington, D.C.: The Catholic Education Press, 1918).

*Catholic National Readers, Books Five and Six* (New York: Benziger Brothers, 1890s).

*The Catholic Youth Fifth and Sixth Readers*, Rena A. Weider, B.S. and Msgr. Charles F. McEvoy, A.M., LL.D. (Chicago: The John C. Winston Company, 1930).

*The Corona Readers, Book 4*, James H. Fassett (Boston: Ginn and Company, 1926).

*De la Salle Readers Fourth, Fifth and Sixth Grade*, Brothers of the Christian Schools (New York: St. Joseph's Normal Institute, 1915).

*The Ideal Catholic Reader, Fifth Reader*, A Sister of St. Joseph (New York: The MacMillan Company, 1916).

*Literature and Art Books, Book Five*, Bridget Ellen Burke (Boston: Educational Publishing Company, 1909).

*The Marywood Readers: Sunny Skies (Fifth Reader)*, Sister Mary Estelle (New York: The MacMillan Company, 1932).

*Misericordia Readers Fifth Reader*, The Sisters of Mercy (Chicago: Rand McNally & Company, 1928).

*The Rosary Readers Fourth, Fifth and Sixth Reader*, Sister Mary Henry, O.S.D. (Boston: Ginn and Company, 1929-30).

## Additional Student Reading for Fifth Grade

*Bible and Church History*, Sister Anna Louise, S.S.J. (New York: William H. Sadlier, Inc., 1928).

*A Character Calendar*, Sister M. Fidelis, Sister Mary Charitas (S.S.N.D.) (Milwaukee: The Bruce Publishing Company, 1931).

*\*A Child's Garden of Religion Stories*, Rev. P. Henry Matimore, S.T.D. (New York: The Macmillan Company, 1929).

*\*Heroes of God's Church*, Rev. P. Henry Matimore, S.T.D. (New York: The Macmillan Company, 1930).

*Medal Stories (3 volumes)*, Daughters of Charity (Racine: Whitman Publishing Company, 1932-34).

*\*Wonder Stories of God's People*, Rev. P. Henry Matimore, S.T.D. (New York: The Macmillan Company, 1929).

# THE HIGHWAY TO HEAVEN SERIES

*Prepared in the Catechetical Institute of Marquette University*

(In co-operation with a group of Priests and Sisters teaching in the elementary schools)

| GRADE | TEXT | MANUAL<br>CURRICULUM IN RELIGION<br>*(1st to 8th Grade inclusive)* |
|---|---|---|
| 1 | **THE BOOK OF THE HOLY CHILD**<br>By *Sister Mary Bartholomew, O.S.F.*<br>96 pages | First Grade Teachers Plan Book and Manual |
| 2 | **THE LIFE OF MY SAVIOR**<br>By a School Sister of Notre Dame<br>196 pages | Second Grade Teachers Plan Book and Manual |
| 3 | **THE LIFE OF THE SOUL**<br>Prepared in the Catechetical Institute of Marquette University<br>*Edward A. Fitzpatrick, Ph.D.*<br>Educational Director<br>144 pages | Third Grade Teachers Plan Book and Manual |
| 4 | **BEFORE CHRIST CAME**<br>By a School Sister of Notre Dame<br>256 pages | Fourth Grade Teachers Plan Book and Manual |
| 5 | **THE VINE AND THE BRANCHES**<br>By the *Rev. R. G. Bandas, Ph.D.Agg., S.T.D. et M.*<br>and a School Sister of Notre Dame<br>320 pages | Fifth Grade Teachers Plan Book and Manual |
| 6 | **THE SMALL MISSAL** | Workbook for the Missal |
| 7 & 8 | **THE HIGHWAY TO GOD**<br>Prepared in the Catechetical Institute of Marquette University<br>*Edward A. Fitzpatrick, Ph.D.*<br>Educational Director<br>420 pages | Practical Problems in Religion<br>By the *Rev. R. G. Bandas, Ph.D.Agg., S.T.D. et M.*<br>(Answers problems in text) |